THE
HOME
REPAIR

EMERGENCY HANDBOOK

Also by Gene Schnaser
Trade Secrets

THE HOME REPAIR EMERGENCY HANDBOOK

Gene Schnaser

Taylor Publishing Company
Dallas, Texas

Notice: Every effort has been made to ensure that the information contained herein is accurate. However, due to the variability of local conditions, skills, and materials, Taylor Publishing and the author assume no responsibility for any injuries suffered or damages or other losses incurred during or as the result of following this information. All potential consequences, including safety factors, should be carefully considered before taking any action, based on immediate circumstances. If any question exists regarding proper procedures, consult local experts.

Published by Taylor Publishing Company
1550 West Mockingbird Lane
Dallas, Texas 75235

Designed by Gary Hespenheide

Illustrations by Deborah J. Jackson-Jones

Library of Congress Cataloging-in-Publication Data

Schnaser, Gene.
     The home repair emergency handbook / Gene Schnaser.
        p.   cm.
     Includes index.
     ISBN 0-87833-797-0
     1. Dwellings—Maintenance and repair—Amateurs' manuals. 2. Household appliances—
Maintenance and repair—Amateurs' manuals.
     I. Title.
TH4817.S28   1992
643'.7—dc20   92-14253
                                                                                                        CIP

Printed in the United States of America

10 9 8 7 6 5 4 3 2 1

LUKE SKYWALKER:
"Okay, I'll give it a try."

YODA:
"No! Try not. Do—or do not. There is no try."

THE EMPIRE STRIKES BACK

ACKNOWLEDGMENTS

The author extends his appreciation to the following companies and organizations for their assistance in researching the material presented in this book: Armstrong World Industries, Inc.; Artesian Industries; AT&T; Dura-Vent Corporation; Federal Emergency Management Agency; Federal Insurance Administration; Fluidmaster, Inc.; Garage Door Council; General Electric Company; Genova, Inc.; Georgia-Pacific; Gypsum Association; Honeywell Inc.; Iowa State University Cooperative Extension Service; Jenn-Air Corporation; Johnson Wax; Kentile Floors; Maytag Company; McGraw-Edison Company; Melard Mfg. Corporation; Minnesota Agricultural Extension Service; Minnesota Department of Health; Minnesota Department of Public Safety; National Flood Insurance Program; National Oak Flooring Manufacturers' Association; Northern States Power Company; Pittway Corporation; Sears, Roebuck and Co.; Skil Corporation; Stanley Tools, Division of Stanley Works; United States Department of Agriculture; United States Department of Commerce, National Bureau of Standards; United States Geological Survey; U.S. West Communications; Whirlpool Corporation, and the many others who assisted in smaller but significant ways.

CONTENTS

Home Appliances — 91

Home Interiors — 111

Home Exteriors — 139

Home Pest Control

INTRODUCTION

About Home Emergencies

This is one of the most valuable books you have ever bought for yourself, a loved-one, or a friend. It's been assembled for the thousands of first-time home buyers, as well as the ever-increasing number of single parents, and others who need help in understanding the technology used in today's homes. It not only includes valuable lifesaving facts, but also gives you a head start on solving a full array of the most common problems encountered in American homes.

Leaking pipes, appliances that quit working, plugged-up toilets, bats in the attic—the list of emergencies that can foul up your home systems is nearly endless. But what is a home emergency? Simply put, it is an event that endangers those who live in the home, or makes the home uninhabitable (or at least uncomfortable). It also can be a problem that renders the home structure or its many systems inoperable, or makes their long-term use unlikely.

Once you start counting, there are nearly two dozen home emergencies that call for immediate action. Other problems may or may not be emergencies—depending on the problem and your coping skills—and usually can be remedied over a longer period of time. This book includes nearly 120 entries addressing specific home problems; each entry giving you helpful background facts, tips on what to do, special advice you should know, and helpful hints to help you get things back to normal.

Because most home systems are mechanical or electrical in nature, they are prone to breakdowns, malfunctions, and complete outright failure. Enjoying the benefits of increasingly sophisticated technology in our homes comes with a price. That price is taking the time, and making the effort, to learn how to live in harmony with these high-tech systems. This book will help guide you through typical home problems, ranging from snapping water heaters to sticking doors, that can make your life miserable.

What you might consider an emergency, your neighbor next door might dismiss as a simple technological malfunction. Your reaction depends on whether you know how to correct, or at least minimize, the malfunctions that occur every day in homes across America. You may be able to correct the cause of many potential emergencies yourself,

1

depending on your experience and the tools you have or wish to buy. In some cases, the information here will help you avoid paying professional technicians' costly service charges. In other cases, it will help you understand the problem so you will be able to talk with professionals more intelligently.

You don't have to become a housing expert to learn how to handle small, common household emergencies. And your payback will be much more than the money you save. By taking care of things that can lead to trouble, you will enjoy the benefits of living in a home where everything works. As simple maintenance is done on a regular schedule, you will have fewer mental notes to clutter your mind. Even more important, by becoming a better manager of your home's systems, you will be able to prevent emergencies that could cost you thousands of dollars.

Home emergencies are almost always unexpected and difficult to plan for. They have something else in common: Most can be avoided if you just know how to turn things off in your home. If the people in your household know how to turn off the main electrical switch, the main water valve, and the main gas valve, what ordinarily might become a potential disaster is easily reduced to a small problem.

Take the time soon to find out where these critical shutoffs are located in your home. Identify them clearly, and write down their locations in the Quick-Reference Emer-

gency Guide at the front of this book. Then get the members of your household together and show them where they are. Also take the time to assemble the phone numbers to call for emergency services for the electrical, plumbing, and heating and cooling systems in your home— preferably companies who offer service on a 24-hour basis. Then make sure everyone in your home knows where to find these numbers. The time spent doing this may pay off handsomely in the future.

Just about any home project has the potential to cause serious injury if safety precautions are not taken. Work on electrical systems and appliances requires that specific precautions be taken. All individuals are responsible for determining their own capability to safely complete any repairs or improvements, and to study and use required and necessary safety procedures.

In most areas, building permits and inspections are required when modifications to the mechanical system of the home are made. Comply with local requirements and view inspections as necessary to be certain that repairs and improvements were done correctly and safely.

Do not work on any project unless you thoroughly understand the required safety procedures and precautions. When working on appliances, for example, always disconnect the electrical power by removing the power cord plug from its electrical outlet before beginning any work. Make sure you know where the fuses or circuit breakers are located in your home, and how to disconnect the power to all circuits by using the main switch, or how to shut off specific circuits by disconnecting fuses or circuit breakers.

To disconnect fuses, carefully unscrew the fuse from the service box; to disconnect circuit breakers, move the switch to the "off" position. To confirm that you have disconnected the right circuit, turn an appliance on or plug a working table lamp into the outlet that the appliance was plugged into. If the appliance or light turns on, you have disconnected the wrong circuit and must keep disconnecting circuits until the appliance or light goes off.

This book is meant to serve as a first-step resource for solving home problems. If you are inexperienced, or have questions regarding safety precautions or repair procedures, be sure to consult local experts and detailed owner manuals.

QUICK-REFERENCE HOME EMERGENCY GUIDE

Be prepared! By noting important phone numbers and other essential information on these pages, you could save valuable time when an emergency occurs in your home. Take the time to fill out this emergency information and show the rest of your family these pages. Keep this book in a handy, accessible place so it can be used by anyone.

Note: Use this opportunity to acquaint yourself and your family with all power, gas, oil, water, and other shutoffs for your home. Place large, clearly marked tie-on tags on all shutoffs where practical. Doing so could help others keep minor problems from turning into major disasters.

For Emergencies, Call 911.

Our Address is ....

Our Phone Number is ....

Family Work, School, and Neighbor Numbers

Parent/Guardian At Work ....

Parent/Guardian At Work ....

Children's Schools ....

....

Friend/Neighbor ....

Relative/Friend (Out-of-Town) ....

....

Fire, Police, and Medical Emergency Numbers

Fire Department ....

Police Department ....

Sheriff Department ....

Hospital ....

Ambulance ....

Poison Control Center ....

Family Doctor ....

Other Doctors ....

....

Home Utilities Emergency Numbers

Electrical Power Company ....

Natural Gas Company ....

Water Department ....

Heating Oil Supplier ....

Liquid Propane or Bottle Gas Supplier ....

Others ....

....

Repair Service Emergency Numbers

Heating Equipment Service ....

Air-Conditioning Service ....

Telephone Repair Service ....

Cable Television Service ....

Plumbers ....

....

....

Electricians ....

....

....

Appliance Repair Services ....

....

....

....

Other Repair Services . . . .
. . . .
. . . .
. . . .

Emergency Switch and Valve Locations

Electrical Main Switch . . . .
. . . .
. . . .

Load Center Switches . . . .
. . . .

❑ Furnace Power . . . .
❑ Air-Conditioner Power . . . .
❑ Water Heater Power . . . .
❑ Range/Oven Power . . . .
❑ Clothes Dryer Power . . . .
❑ Other Power Switches . . . .
. . . .
. . . .

Gas Main Valve . . . .
. . . .
. . . .

Secondary Gas Shutoffs . . . .
. . . .

❑ Furnace Gas . . . .
❑ Water Heater Gas . . . .
❑ Range/Oven Gas . . . .
❑ Clothes Dryer Gas . . . .
❑ Other Gas Shutoffs . . . .
. . . .

. . . .

Water Main Valve . . . .

. . . .

. . . .

Secondary Water Shutoffs . . . .

. . . .

. . . .

Oil Line Shutoffs . . . .

Liquid Propane or Bottle Gas Shutoffs . . . .

. . . .

Other Emergency Notes

Note below other critical information that would be helpful to others in your absence.

Emergency Supply Locations . . . .

. . . .

. . . .

. . . .

Fire Extinguisher Locations . . . .

. . . .

. . . .

. . . .

Family Fire Escape Plan . . . .

. . . .

. . . .

. . . .

. . . .

. . . .

. . . .

Additional Notes . . . .

. . . .

. . . .

. . . .

. . . .

. . . .

. . . .

THE WELL-STOCKED TOOLBOX

The equipment you will need for home projects depends on which ones you intend to tackle. You can progressively add to your collection as you tackle various jobs around the home. If, for example, you decide to install or repair wallboard for the first time, you may already have a hammer, level, carpenter's square, and utility knife, but will need to buy special taping knives and a keyhole saw. If you plan to work on the electrical system, specialized testers and cable- and wire-stripping tools will be essential. If you need to fix a plugged-up plumbing system, purchasing a rubber-cup plunger, drain-clearing flexible auger, or a toilet (closet) auger may be necessary. If you are working with plumbing pipes, crescent-type adjustable wrenches, a vice grip-type wrench and a pair of pipe wrenches (one smaller, one larger) may be essential. In all cases, consider personal safety gear, such as safety glasses (or goggles), gloves, and ear protection, your first priority when buying equipment. Also provide enough light, either with clip-on task lamps or with trouble lights, so you will be able to see what you are doing at all times.

Use the following lists as general guidelines for getting started and building your basic collection of tools. To save money in the long run, tool experts recommend buying the best tools you can afford, so that subsequent purchases will add to your collection instead of replacing tools you already had.

The Basic Toolbox

Hand Tools
19-inch portable toolbox
30-foot tape rule
16-oz. curved claw hammer
Screwdriver set or four-way rachet
    screwdriver
$\frac{3}{8}$-inch socket set
Flat combination wrenches
6-inch slip-joint pliers
General purpose cross-cut handsaw
Mitre saw and mitre box
Utility knife
24-inch level
Chalk line
Awl
Carpenter's square

Power Tools
$\frac{3}{8}$-inch electric drill, variable speeds
Cordless power screwdriver
Cordless, $\frac{3}{8}$-inch power wrench
Jig (or sabre) saw

The Intermediate Toolbox

Hand Tools
20-inch (or larger) portable toolbox or tool chest
16-oz. hammer with steel handle
¼-inch and ½-inch socket sets with deep sockets
Screwdrivers of all sizes
Needle-nose pliers
Heavy-duty utility knife
Mitre box with 10° and 90° range
C-clamps and bar clamps
48-inch level
Small pry bars (at least one pair)

Power Tools
10-inch benchtop table saw
Scroll saw
Benchtop drill press
Combination belt/disc sander
⅜-inch cordless or electric drill
⅜-inch hammer drill, variable speeds
5½-inch trim saw
Reciprocating saw
Belt sander

The Advanced Toolbox

Hand Tools
32-inch portable toolbox
Tool chest and/or cabinet
100-foot tape rule
16-oz. hammer with fiberglass handle
Triangular grip screwdriver, professional quality
Diagonal cutting pliers
Heavy-duty utility knife
Crosscut saw with 10 or more teeth per inch
Wallboard saw
Hacksaw
72-inch level
Rafter, combination, and try squares

Power Tools
½-inch electric drill
Cordless drill/driver
Miter saw
Plate joiner
Laminate trimmer
Router
Specialty sanders

CRITICAL HOME EMERGENCIES

● ● ● ● ● ● ● ● ● ● ● ● ●

1
Fire Inside Home

Problem: Smoke alarms sound, or fire is discovered in home.

Background: In case of a fire emergency, don't panic; stay calm. Your safe escape may depend on clear thinking. Get out of the house as quickly as possible, following any previously planned escape route. Don't stop to collect anything or to get dressed. Feel the doors to see if they are hot. If they are not, open them carefully. If they are hot, don't open them and use an alternate escape route. Stay close to the floor because smoke and hot gases rise. Cover your nose and mouth with a cloth (wet if possible) and take short, shallow breaths. Keep doors and windows closed, opening them only if necessary for escape. Call the fire department as soon as possible from outside your house. Never go back inside a burning building.

What to do: If fire does not appear to be present, check entry 2. It's smart to develop a family escape plan and practice it with your entire family, including small children. Draw a floor plan of your home, and find two ways to exit from every room. There should be one way to get out of each bedroom without opening the door. Explain to children what smoke detector alarms mean, and teach them how to leave the home by themselves if necessary. Show them how to check doors to determine whether they are hot before opening them, how to stay close to the floor and crawl if necessary, and how to use an alternate exit if the door is hot and should not be opened.

Decide on a meeting place a safe distance from your home, and make sure your children understand they should wait for you there if a fire occurs. Hold fire drills at least every 6 months and know where to go to call the fire department from outside your home. Keep emergency equipment, such as fire extinguishers, in the house and teach your family how to use them properly.

Special advice: In addition to installing smoke detectors, providing fire extinguishers, and developing an escape plan, follow good fire prevention practices. Use smoking materials properly and never smoke in bed. Keep matches and cigarette lighters from children. Store flammable materials in proper containers and never use them near open flames or sparks. Keep electrical appliances in good condition and don't overload electrical circuits. Also keep stoves, fireplaces, chimneys and barbecue grills free of grease, and make sure they are used properly, away from combustible materials. Make certain portable heaters and open flames, such as candles, are not used near combustible materials. Do not allow rubbish to accumulate.

Helpful hint: Contact your local fire department for more ideas about how to make your home safer from fires, and how to plan your family's escape.

● ● ●

2 Smoke Detector Sounds

Problem: Smoke detector goes off or chirps when no fire or smoke is present.

Background: Smoke detectors that make a loud continuous sound, when the test button has not been pushed, have sensed smoke or combustion particles in the air. *The alarm horn is a warning of a possibly serious situation and requires your immediate attention.* (See entry 1.) Although detectors offer invaluable protection, they can also make noise when no emergency exists. This may be due to improper installation, low batteries, or dust buildup.

What to do: If detectors are interconnected, check all installation locations for smoke or fire. If the detector beeps about once a minute, it may be signalling that the unit's battery is weak and needs replacement. Replace with new battery immediately. If the detector is hardwired (connected to the home's electrical system), check for smoke or fire in all locations. If none exist, turn off the circuit breaker that controls the alarm and check the detectors. Dirt and dust can build up on the unit's sensing chamber, making it overly sensitive. After batteries are removed, or the power has been shut off, the sensing chamber can be cleaned with a soft brush vacuum attachment; detector covers can be washed by hand using a damp cloth and dried with a lint-free cloth. Replace batteries, or turn power back on, and test unit for operation.

Special advice: Often alarms that are a nuisance result from improper installation. Ideally, detectors should be installed at least 20 feet away from areas where combustion particles (by-products of burning)

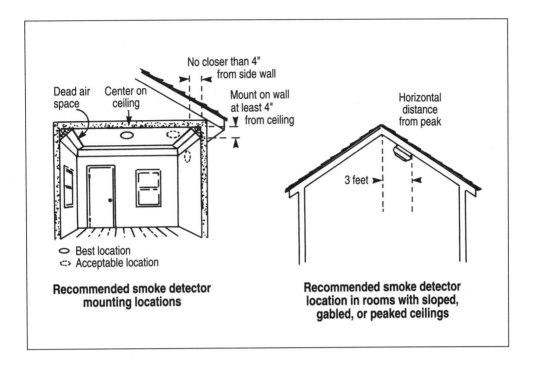

Dead air space

Center on ceiling

No closer than 4" from side wall

Mount on wall at least 4" from ceiling

Horizontal distance from peak

3 feet

○ Best location
⊂⊃ Acceptable location

Recommended smoke detector mounting locations

Recommended smoke detector location in rooms with sloped, gabled, or peaked ceilings

are present. These areas may include: kitchens with few windows or poor ventilation; garages where there may be vehicle exhaust; anywhere near furnaces, hot water heaters, or space heaters. Keep detectors 10 feet away from bathrooms, where condensation can activate alarms, and at least 5 feet away from fluorescent lights, where electrical noise can cause detectors to sound. Insects crawling into a detector's sensing chamber can also cause false alarms. Check the owner's manual or instruction sheet for other areas to avoid, including those where air streams are present, and areas that are damp, cold, hot, drafty, or dusty.

Helpful hint: Only temporarily disconnect a hard-wired detector or remove batteries from a battery-operated detector to stop an annoying alarm. Manufacturers recommend units be tested weekly by pushing on the test button until horn sounds. (Don't use an open flame to test a detector or "aerosol" spray smoke detector testers. Flames may damage the unit and chemicals can change the unit's sensitivity or impair its function.) If a unit fails to test properly, have it repaired by the manufacturer or replace it. Batteries should be replaced with recommended types annually, or sooner if a unit beeps. Detectors that are more than 10 years old should be replaced.

•••

3 Appliance on Fire

Problem: Flames or smoke are coming from appliance.

Background: If an appliance doesn't work correctly, or if it gives even the slightest shock, disconnect it and get it repaired. Insulation makes appliance cords safe. Replace cords that are worn, broken, or brittle from age or overheating because they can cause a dangerous short circuit and fire (see entry 27). Avoid connecting several appliances through an extension cord, or using octopus-type (multiple outlet) plugs. Run cords in safe, out-of-the-way places.

What to do: If you discover a fire in any appliance, unplug it if possible, or turn off the power at the appliance's circuit breaker. Call the fire department and explain that there is an electrical fire, and alert anyone else in the home. Don't put water on the flame; use a fire extinguisher recommended for electrical fires (see below).

Special advice: Only fire extinguishers rated for class C fires and marked with the letter "C" should be used in and around live electrical equipment such as appliances, radios, and TV sets. (Class A fires are those fueled by wood, fabric, paper, rubber, and most plastics; class B fires are fueled by flammable liquids such as oil, gasoline, paint, or grease.) Two kinds of dry-chemical extinguishers are offered for home use: one rated "Multipurpose A:B:C," which uses monoammonium phosphate against all three classes of fires, and another which uses sodium bicarbonate against class B and class C fires.

Helpful hint: Good locations for fire extinguishers include: the corridor near the door of a bedroom; the end wall cabinet next to a kitchen door; in the hall near the living room; by the tool rack near a shop exit; and the wall close to the doors of either a garage or boat house.

●●●

4 Chimney Overheated or on Fire

Problem: Fire in fireplace or wood stove overheats chimney or ignites fire in chimney, accompanied by a loud roaring sound.

Background: A common cause of fires is the over-firing of a stove or fireplace, so that it becomes overheated. This often is the result of building a fire that is too large or too hot. Another cause is an internal fire in the chimney, resulting from an accumulation of soot and tar inside of the chimney. Often internal chimney fires are accelerated in high-efficiency stoves that have controlled drafts and a limited air supply. The buildup is highly flammable and may ignite. Chimney fires can be frightening, and temperatures inside the chimney may reach up to as high as 3,000°F, creating a tremendous updraft that causes a roar.

What to do: The average chimney fire has a duration of 5 minutes or less. Unfortunately, other than calling the fire department, not much can be done during a chimney fire. Extinguish the original fire, if possible. (Some experts suggest dumping large amounts of coarse salt on the fire, then holding a wet blanket over the hearth opening to keep air from entering the chimney.) Do not run water into the hot chimney because this may crack the flue liner or bricks.

Special advice: After a chimney fire has been extinguished, the fire department will inspect your home to make sure it has not been damaged. Do not use the fireplace or stove after a chimney fire until it has been inspected by a chimney expert. To minimize the risk of chimney fires, do not use a fireplace or stove for burning large amounts of paper scraps or wrappings, corrugated boxes, wood shavings, Christmas trees, or wood that contains flammable adhesives (such as plywood or paneling). These materials can burn at temperatures high enough to make chimney damage likely. As a general rule, don't use more than three or four full-sized logs in your

fireplace or other wood-burning device, and have the chimney inspected and cleaned regularly.

Helpful hint: Chemical cleaners can be used to help inhibit soot buildup. (Common rock salt, thrown into the chimney, will not do the job.) Deposits in a chimney can vary from soft and fluffy ash to rock-hard, almost crystalline material. Consider hiring a professional chimney sweep to do the job.

● ● ●

5 Gas Smell in Home

Problem: Natural gas or propane gas smell is detected in home, or in particular area of appliances.

Background: An odorant is added to natural gas and propane gas to alert people of its presence. Gas buildup can be extremely dangerous and should be taken very seriously. Gas leaks, which can result from a number of causes, can produce tremendous explosions, so it is wise to be overly cautious.

What to do: If you smell a strong gas odor upon returning to your home, do not enter. Call for help from a neighbor's phone. If you smell gas within any area of your home, do not try to light any appliance. If faint gas odor is detected, put out any smoking materials, don't turn on any light switches, don't use any phone in the home. Shut off any valves to appliances suspected of leaking the gas, then call a technician. However, if you are in doubt or if the gas odor is strong, leave the home immediately, call your gas supplier from a neighbor's phone, and follow their instructions. If you can't reach the gas supplier, call the fire department or 911.

Special advice: Liquid propane (LP) gas is heavier than air. If there is a leak in a propane system, the gas will settle near the floor. Basements, crawl spaces, skirted areas under mobile homes (even when ventilated), closets, and areas below ground level, can serve as pockets for accumulated gas. Before attempting to light or relight a pilot light, or turning on a nearby electrical switch, be absolutely sure there is no accumulated propane gas in the area by sniffing at floor level in the vicinity of any appliance.

Helpful hint: Be especially cautious about gas leaks whenever new gas appliances have been installed. Check all gas pipes and fittings for leaks with a soapy water solution. Before lighting any newly installed appliance, factory fittings on appliances should be checked by a qualified technician.

● ● ●

6 Gas Detector Sounds

Problem: Alarm designed to detect presence of gas leaks goes off.

Background: Special alarms are available to detect natural gas or liquid propane (LP) gas leaks which could build up to concentrations that could result in explosions or flash fires. Similar to smoke detectors in appearance, they are designed to sound before dangerous levels have been reached, giving you time to correct the problem or vacate the premises.

What to do: If your alarm sounds, take it seriously and immediately check for the odor of gas and for the cause. Situations that can result in gas leaks include:

1) attempting to relight the furnace when the electricity is off
2) pilot lights on furnaces, gas dryers, or water heaters have gone out or have blown out
3) chimney or flue malfunctions which return unburned gases to the basement
4) broken or cracked gas lines or fittings caused by the movement or jarring of appliances or by metal fatigue
5) malfunctions of gas safety valves which should shut off gas when trouble occurs

6) seepage into the basement of natural gas found in the earth, or broken gas mains in the street, which allow gas to enter the basement along water or gas pipes.

Also check the electrical boxes of appliances for overheating. *If none of the potential problems listed above exist, vacate the premises and call the fire or gas company.* (See entry 5.)

Because of the way gas detectors work, false alarms can occur if the unit is installed beyond furnace areas where they can be affected by hydrocarbon gases that are found in items such as hair sprays, cleaning products, paint, cooking odors, and aerosol products. Alarms can also sound if the basement has been painted or fumigated recently, if furniture is being refinished, if cleaning is being done with flammable materials, or if gasoline or flammable liquids are being dangerously stored in open cans.

Special advice: Gas detectors are not intended to detect small concentrations of gas trapped by the walls of the furnace. (To avoid triggering an explosion, always open furnace doors and air out the area before trying to relight pilot lights.) A detector may have sensor lights, indicating that it is plugged in and operational. Gas alarms should be tested at least once a month by briefly holding either an unlit butane lighter or cotton dipped in alcohol under the sensor opening. If the alarm beeps, instead of sounding continuously, it indi-

cates there is a problem and that the unit should be serviced.

Helpful hint: Gas detectors should never be plugged into outlets operated by a wall switch. To detect natural gas, detectors are normally mounted 6 inches to 12 inches from the ceiling and about 4 inches to 12 feet from gas appliances. To detect propane gas, which is heavier than air, the units are normally mounted 6 inches to 12 inches from the floor.

● ● ●

7 Gas Appliance Venting Faulty

Problem: Inadequate air supply within home.

Background: Gas appliances such as furnaces, water heaters, space heaters, and gas logs, must be connected to a flue vented to the outdoors and have an adequate fresh-air supply. If vents, flues, or chimneys are not kept clean and in good repair, toxic carbon monoxide can accumulate (see entry 8). Signs that indicate a gas appliance has an inadequate air supply may include indoor condensation, a yellow or wavering flame, soot in your home, a gas smell, overheating, sick houseplants, or a pilot light that keeps going out.

What to do: Turn off the appliance and call a technician if you have any of the symptoms of carbon monoxide poisoning, which include: an aching head, smarting eyes, ringing ears, nausea, weariness, or frequent yawning. If you have weatherized your home with caulk and weather-stripping, and have closed off the normal air flow through walls, attics, windows, and doors, you may need a fresh-air intake duct to provide sufficient oxygen for your furnace. A heating contractor can install one for you.

Special advice: Make sure flues and chimneys are kept clear of debris such as nests, branches, or ivy. Avoid blocking air vents, valves, or controls if you add insulation around the water heater. Don't cover the top of the heater or the space between the floor and heater.

Helpful hint: To make sure your home is safe, hire a qualified heating contractor to inspect and tune up your gas furnace and water heater each year and check any automatic vent dampers in use (see entries 54 and 61).

● ● ●

8 Carbon Monoxide in Home

Problem: Carbon monoxide affects personal health.

Background: Carbon monoxide (CO) is a colorless, odorless, and tasteless gas. Usually carbon dioxide (CO_2) is produced during the combustion of carbon-containing, or organic, material, such as natural gas, oil, and wood. But if enough oxygen is not present, CO is formed instead of CO_2. Any gas, oil, kerosene or wood-powered appliance, or combustion product has the potential to produce carbon monoxide. Examples include wood stoves, fireplaces, space heaters, charcoal grills, furnaces, water heaters, boilers, and gas cooking ranges. (If adequate combustion air is provided, and the appliance is properly installed and maintained, the small amounts of carbon monoxide generated can be safely vented to the outside.) Other sources include burning cigarettes; combustion appliances, such as a hibachi, used indoors; a cooking stove, used to heat a room; a blocked or leaky chimney; a cracked or corroded heat exchanger; combustion air backdrafts that spill back into the home instead of going out the chimney, vent, or flue.

What to do: Each year as many as 10,000 United States residents seek medical treatment for carbon monoxide poisoning. Typical symptoms of exposure to low levels of carbon monoxide include headaches, dizziness, drowsiness, nausea, and vomiting. (Long-term exposure to low levels has also been known to cause chest pains.) Exposure to high levels can result in unconsciousness and death. Some people are more sensitive to carbon monoxide than others. If your home has gas appliances, and you or other family members are experiencing some of the above symptoms, check your appliances and see your doctor to be tested. If you believe your furnace or other heating appliances are releasing carbon monoxide, consult a heating or ventilation contractor or the company that provides your heating fuel. A visual inspection may identify the cause.

The first step in preventing problems is hiring a qualified technician to install fuel-burning equipment or to convert an appliance from using one type of fuel to using another. Never burn charcoal inside the house in a grill, hibachi, or fireplace. Don't heat or warm a room with a gas oven, and don't use a stove or fireplace that is not properly vented. Don't run a car engine, lawn mower, or other combustion engine in a closed garage. Set up a maintenance schedule with a qualified technician to inspect your furnace or boiler. See entries 7 and 54.

Special advice: Acceptable levels of carbon monoxide in the home is considered 9 parts per million (ppm) or less. Monitoring and testing services are available through private testing labs and safety supply stores. Passive monitors, about $10, change color when elevated CO_2 levels are detected. Electronic monitors, similar to smoke detectors (about $70 to $150), sound an alarm.

Helpful hint: Canadian studies show most carbon monoxide poisoning problems are related to poor maintenance; damaged chimneys, vents, and flues; and improper installation of equipment. One out of four cases results from the backdraft of furnace and water heater gasses. The backdraft may be due to excessive exhaust, inadequate air supply, and extreme airtightness of the home.

●●●

9 Power Supply Is Cut Off

Problem: Electrical power is cut off to home because of storms, tornadoes, floods, or other mechanical failures.

Background: Fortunately most power outages today are only temporary. If a storm knocks down a power line near your home, stay away from it. Call the fire or police department for help in keeping people away, and report the downed line to your electric utility immediately.

What to do: If the power goes off, unplug or turn off major appliances in use when power went out. This will help eliminate the need for a large surge of electric power when the service returns. Such a surge could damage your TV or appliances and the electric distribution system in addition to prolonging the outage. Leave at least one light switched on so you will know when the power is restored. When power returns, wait a few minutes before turning on lights and appliances, then turn them on one at a time. If the power goes off again right after it has been restored, check the fuses and circuit breakers to be sure they haven't blown or tripped. To help keep food cold as long as possible, do not open freezer or refrigerator doors unless absolutely necessary. If outage cuts off heat in cold weather, see entry 10.

Special advice: As with most emergencies, it's best to be prepared beforehand. Assemble emergency supplies, such as candles, matches, fresh batteries, a flashlight, and a battery-powered radio, in a special cabinet or drawer in your home.

Helpful hint: If lighting your home with candles or oil lamps during an outage, placing them near light-colored walls or mirrors at shoulder height can increase illumination. Be careful to keep open flames out of drafts, away from draperies and upholstery, and out of the reach of children.

●●●

10 Fuel Supply Is Cut Off

Problem: Home's fuel supply is cut off or diminished.

Background: Power outages, as well as fuel outages, can immobilize the heating and cooking systems in the home. If electricity is off, see entry 9. If you suspect the gas supply has been cut off, first check the pilot lights and other gas appliances to see if they are working. If they are not, contact the utility company. If you suspect a gas leak problem, follow emergency procedures and don't use matches, electrical appliances, light switches, a flashlight, or smoke cigarettes (see entry 5). If oil heating system doesn't work, check to see if there is fuel in the tank and whether the furnace blower is getting power. In all cases, contact your utility or service technician if you suspect other problems with furnaces (see entry 54).

What to do: Until heating systems are restored to operation, you can supplement home heating with a fireplace or with propane or kerosene heaters. However, *use extreme caution with auxiliary heaters.* They need good ventilation. Such heaters will not provide safe heat for an entire house, but they can help keep the indoor temperature above the freezing point. If you use campstoves or canned-heat products for cooking during an emergency, you must also *ventilate your home carefully.* Never use a hibachi or charcoal-burning grills indoors. They produce carbon monoxide and other dangerous fumes.

Special advice: If a power outage during freezing weather cuts off heat, water pipes can freeze and later burst. If heat is off for a few hours, accessible pipes can be wrapped with newspaper or other material. In extremely cold weather, leave faucets slightly open and shut off water valve on toilet and flush until bowl and tank are empty. If heat is off longer than a couple of days, turn off main valve or water pump, water heater and/or water heating furnace. Save some water for emergency use, then open all faucets and drain the water heater and all pipes by opening the drain valves. If pipes freeze, shut off main water supply, open faucets fully and remove any pipe-wrappings (see entry 42).

Helpful hint: Follow the manufacturer's owner manuals, or call your gas company, for instructions on how to shut off gas appliances in an emergency, and how to relight pilot lights. *If a pilot light won't light or if you smell gas, call your gas company or a service technician.* If only the furnace is not working, never use a gas kitchen range as a space heater. This can damage the range and produce dangerous carbon monoxide gas.

●●●

11 Physical Contact with Electricity

Problem: Person suffers electrical shock.

Background: Electrical shock can paralyze chest muscles, making it impossible to breathe. Call immediately for medical help. If a victim is no longer in contact with the source of the electricity, and is not breathing, immediately give mouth-to-mouth resuscitation if possible. When the victim begins to breathe, treat for traumatic shock. Keep warm with clothing or blanket, and position feet higher than head to help blood reach the brain.

What to do: If you find someone in contact with live electricity indoors, don't touch the person since the electricity could travel through them to you as well. Shut off the power by pulling the plug, turning the switch, or turning off the power at the circuit breaker. If you can't turn off the power, you can try to free the victim using a dry rope or stick that won't conduct electricity to you *(use extreme caution and don't use anything wet or made from metal to move the victim).* Call for emergency medical assistance. If you find someone in contact with a live wire outdoors, call the fire or police department for emergency medical assistance. Then also call your electric utility company to tell them the exact location of the victim so they can immediately shut off the power.

Special advice: Power lines downed by storms or accidents are very dangerous; the body can act as a lightning rod and carry the current to the ground. Be alert for power lines, especially when working with scaffolds, ladders and tools, when installing antennas, when trimming trees or flying kites. Call the utility company to help locate underground conduits before digging in your yard. Don't use electric mowers or power tools on a wet surface, and keep appliances away from water, including tubs and showers.

Helpful hint: Call for help if you must work near utility poles or power lines. Tennis shoes or work gloves will not protect you from electrical shock. Power company employees use special precautions, such as rubber protectors, insulating rubber safety gloves and hard hats, plus years of training, to keep themselves safe.

NATURE'S EMERGENCIES

● ● ● ● ● ● ● ● ● ● ● ● ●

12 Tornado Threatens Home

Problem: Tornadoes are predicted or present in area of the home.

Background: Tornadoes are formed by severe thunderstorms, most often in spring and summer. They are nature's most violent and erratic storms. A tornado can travel for miles along the ground, lift, and suddenly change directions and strike again. Basic safety rules include:

1) keep alert and watch for changing weather conditions
2) take shelter immediately when you hear a tornado warning or see a funnel cloud
3) know where shelter is before you need it.

Learn your community's warning signals. A tornado watch is announced when weather conditions are favorable for the formation of tornadoes. A tornado warning is announced when a funnel cloud is sighted or indicated by radar.

What to do: There is little you can do to protect your home or workplace from the strength of tornado winds. But you can increase your chances of survival by knowing which locations may be safer than others. In conventional homes, a basic rule is to avoid standing or sitting near windows; an exploding window can injure or kill. Don't take time to open windows—just get to shelter immediately. The safest place in the home is the interior part of the basement, preferably under something sturdy like a table. Stay out from under heavy objects like pianos or refrigerators located on the floor above. If you have no basement, or can't get there, go to an inside room with no windows—like a closet, hallway, or bathroom—on the lowest floor of the home. For added protection, sit under something that is strong, like a workbench or heavy table. If possible, cover your body with a blanket or sleeping bag, and protect your head with anything available, even your hands.

Do not stay in a mobile home during a tornado. Even homes with a secure tie-down system can't withstand the force of tornado winds. Plan ahead and make arrangements to stay with someone who has a basement if a tornado watch is issued. If a tornado warning is given, leave a mobile home and seek shelter nearby. If you are in a car, do not try to outrun a tornado; vehicles are easily tossed by the winds. If you see a tornado, stop and get out. Seek shelter away from the car in a nearby ditch or ravine; do not go into a grove of trees or crawl under your vehicle. Lie flat and put your arms over your head.

Special advice: Long-span buildings are especially dangerous since the entire roof structure is usually supported only by the outside walls. If you are caught in an open building like a shopping mall, civic center, indoor pool, theater or gymnasium during a tornado, go into the restroom if possible. In larger buildings, restrooms are usually made of concrete blocks. If there is no time to go anywhere, try to stand up against something that will support or deflect falling debris. In schools, hospitals, nursing homes and office buildings, move to the innermost portions on the lowest possible floor. Avoid windows and glass doorways and don't use elevators; the power may go off and you could

be trapped. Remember to protect your head.

Helpful hint: Keep your family together and wait for help to arrive. After a tornado, don't go into damaged buildings; they may collapse completely. If your home appears undamaged, carefully check for gas leaks (by smelling for gaslike odors) or other utility line breaks. If the lights are out, use a flashlight only; do not use a match, lighter or any open flame. Also see entries 14 and 17.

●●●

13 Flood Threatens Home

Problem: Floodwater threatens the family, the home and its contents, and the community.

Background: In flood situations, the safety of your family is the most important consideration. Since floodwater can rise very rapidly, you should be prepared to evacuate before the water level reaches your property. Before a flood threatens, learn the safest route from your home or office to high, safe ground should you need to evacuate in a hurry. Also keep a portable radio, emergency cooking equipment, and flashlights in working order.

What to do: Tune a battery-powered radio to a local station, and follow all emergency instructions. If you're caught in the house by suddenly rising water, move to the second floor and, if necessary, to the roof. Take warm clothing, a flashlight and a portable radio with you. Then wait for help; don't try to swim to safety. Rescue teams will be looking for you. When outside, remember that floods are deceptive. Try to avoid flooded areas, and don't attempt to walk through floodwater that is more than knee deep.

If (and only if) time permits, turn off all utilities at the main power switch and close the main gas valve if evacuation appears necessary. Don't touch any wet electrical equipment. Move valuable papers and possessions to upper floors or higher elevations. Fill tubs, sinks and buckets with clean water, in case regular supplies are contaminated. (You can sanitize these containers by first rinsing with bleach.) Board up windows, or protect them with storm shutters or tape to prevent broken glass from flying. Bring in outdoor possessions that might be swept away, or tie them down securely.

If it's safe to evacuate by car, stock the car with nonperishable foods (like canned goods), a plastic container of water, blankets, first aid kit, flashlights, dry clothing and any special medication needed by your

family members. Keep the gas tank at least half full since gas pumps won't be working if electricity gets cut off. Don't drive where water is over the roads; parts of the road may already be washed out. If your car stalls in a flooded area, abandon it if you can do so safely since floodwater can rise rapidly and sweep a car and its occupants away. Many deaths have resulted from attempts to move stalled vehicles.

Special advice: If you live in a frequently flooded area, keep materials such as sandbags, plywood, plastic sheeting, and lumber on hand to use to protect your property. Sandbags should not be stacked directly against the outer walls of a building since they can create added pressure on the foundation when they are wet. Also check about eligibility for flood insurance offered through the National Flood Insurance Program. Generally there is a 5-day waiting period before a policy goes into effect, so don't wait until the last minute to apply.

Helpful hint: Make an itemized list of personal property (photos are helpful) to assist an adjuster in settling claims and to help prove uninsured losses, which are tax deductible. Keep your insurance policies and a list of personal property in a safe place outside your home, such as a safety deposit box. Know the name and location of the agents who issued these policies.

For more information on what to do after a flood, see entry 14.

• • •

14 Home Has Been Flooded

Problem: Home has suffered damage from floodwater.

Background: For what to do if a flood is imminent, see entry 13. If your home has been flooded, and you have a flood insurance policy, immediately call the agent or broker who handled it. The agent will submit a loss form to the National Flood Insurance Program and an adjuster will be assigned to inspect your property. Most standard homeowners policies do not cover flood loss. Proceed with immediate cleanup measures after the flood.

Before entering the home, make sure it is not in danger of collapsing. Turn off any outside gas lines at the meter or tank, and let the house air for enough time to remove foul odors or escaping gas.

What to do: When entering a building after a flood, use a battery flashlight instead of an open flame as a light source because gas may still be trapped inside the building. Watch for electrical shorts of live wires before making certain that the main power switch is turned off. Don't turn on any lights or appliances until an electrician has checked the system for short circuits. Cover broken windows and holes in the roof or walls to prevent further weather damage. (Take pictures of the damage done to your home and contents to aid in settling any insurance claims.) Throw out perishable items that pose a health problem, as well as any previously opened medicines that have come in contact with floodwater. Until the public water system has been declared safe, vigorously boil water for drinking and preparing foods for 10 minutes.

Shovel mud out of the building while it is still moist to give walls and floors a chance to dry. Once plastered walls have dried, brush off loose dirt, wash with a mild soap solution, and rinse with clean water. Always start at the bottom and work up, doing ceilings last. When cleaning, pay special attention to heating and plumbing systems. Clean off refrigerators, sofas, and other hard goods and keep until inspected by an adjuster. Any partially damaged items should be dried and aired; the adjuster will make recommendations for repairs or disposal. Move wooden furniture outdoors, but keep out of direct sun to prevent warping. Remove drawers and other moving parts, but do not pry open swollen drawers from the front; instead, remove the backing and push the drawers out. Allow clothing or household fabrics to dry slowly, away from direct heat.

Special advice: Drain and clean flooded basements as soon as possible but be aware that structural damage can occur when water is pumped out too quickly. After the floodwaters around your property have subsided, begin draining the basement in stages; drain about a third of the water volume each day. Mildew can be removed from dry wood with a solution of 4 to 6 table-spoons of trisodium phosphate (TSP), 1 cup liquid chlorine bleach, and 1 gallon of water. Clean metal, then wipe with a kerosene-soaked cloth. Use a light coating of oil on iron to prevent rusting.

Helpful hint: Another method of disinfecting water for drinking or cooking is to mix ½ teaspoon of liquid commercial laundry bleach with 2½ gallons of water, and let stand for 5 minutes before using. The flat taste can be removed by pouring the water from one container to another, or by adding a pinch of salt. In an emergency, water may be acquired by draining a hot water tank or by melting ice cubes.

● ● ●

15 Hurricane Threatens Home

Problem: Major hurricane is heading toward your location, bringing dangerous winds, floods, and storm surges.

Background: While hurricanes are relatively rare events at any one lo-cation, none of the United States coastal areas is immune. Hurricanes are tropical cyclones in which winds reach speeds of 74 miles per hour or more, and blow in a large spiral around a relatively calm center (the eye of the hurricane). Near the center counterclockwise rotating winds may gust to more than 200 miles per hour. Hurricanes that strike the eastern United States originate in the tropical and subtropical North Atlantic Ocean, the Caribbean Sea, and the Gulf of Mexico. Most occur in August, September, and October, but the 6-month period from June 1 to November 30 is considered the Atlantic hurricane season. An aver-age of six Atlantic hurricanes occur each year, and drift gradually to the west-northwest. Initially the storms move forward very slowly in the tropics (about 15 miles per hour), in-creasing in forward speed to some-times more than 50 miles per hour.

What to do: Collect and read gov-ernment and community literature about safety measures. When a hurricane threatens, you need to de-cide whether to evacuate or to ride out the storm at home. If local au-thorities recommend evacuation, leave! Their advice is based on their knowledge of the storm's strength and its potential for death and de-struction. In general, plan to leave if you live on the coastline or offshore islands, if you live in a mobile home, or if you live near a river or in a flood plain.

Make plans before the hurricane season (June). Learn the storm surge history and elevation of your area. Determine safe routes inland, the location of official shelters, and where to move your boat (if you have one) in an emergency. Trim back dead wood from trees, check for loose rain gutters and downspouts. If shutters on your home don't protect windows, keep boards on hand to nail over the windows and cover the glass. When a hurricane watch is issued for your area, check often for official bulletins on radio, TV, or National Oceanic and Atmospheric Administration (NOAA) weather radio. Fuel your car, check mobile home tie-downs, moor or move your small craft to safe shelter, and stock up on canned goods. Also check your supply of special medicines and drugs and batteries for radios and flashlights. Secure lawn furniture and other loose outdoor items. Tape, board, or shutter windows, and wedge sliding glass doors to prevent them from lifting out of their tracks.

When a hurricane warning is issued for your area, stay tuned to radio, TV, or NOAA weather radio for official bulletins. Leave if you are in a mobile home, or if officials advise. Leave in daylight if possible, shut off water and power at mains; take small valuables and papers but travel light. Leave food and water for pets, lock up the home and drive carefully to the nearest designated shelter using the recommended evacuation routes. If you stay home, board up garage and porch doors, move valuables to upper floors, and bring pets inside. Fill containers and bathtub with a supply of water for drinking. Turn the temperature control in the refrigerator to coldest setting and don't open unnecessarily. Use the phone for emergencies only.

Special advice: After the all-clear is announced, drive carefully and watch for dangling electrical wires, weakened roads and bridges, and flooded low spots. Avoid downed power lines and any water in which they may be lying, as well as weakened tree limbs or damaged overhanging boards. Watch for poisonous snakes, which may have been driven from their dens by high water. Don't go sightseeing. Report broken or damaged water, sewer, and electrical lines. Avoid using the phone any more than absolutely necessary (the system will likely be jammed with calls). Use caution when re-entering your home. Check for gas leaks (don't use any flames for light) by smelling for any gaslike odor, and check food and water for spoilage. Don't drink or prepare food with tap water until you are sure it is not contaminated. For more tips on re-entering your home, read entries 14 and 17.

Helpful hint: Beware of the "eye" of the storm. If the eye of the hurricane passes over your area, be aware that the improved weather conditions are temporary, and that the storm conditions will return—sometimes in a few seconds—with winds that come from the opposite direction.

●●●

16 Earthquake Threatens Home

Problem: Home is in earthquake area, or is threatened by earthquake.

Install supports for pipes.

Background: Accurate predictions of earthquakes cannot be made. In the United States, earthquakes occur most often in the western states, but can occur at widely scattered locations across the country. Most casualties result from falling objects and debris, and are caused by partial building collapse, flying glass, overturned fixtures and other furniture and appliances, fires from broken chimneys or broken gas lines, fallen power lines, and drastic actions taken in moments of panic. Consider the suggestions below for measures you can take before and during an earthquake. If your home has suffered earthquake damage, see entry 17.

What to do: Besides supporting community efforts to prepare for an earthquake, check your home for earthquake hazards. Bolt down or provide other strong support for water heaters and other gas appliances, because fires can result from broken gas lines and appliance connections. (Use flexible connections wherever possible.) Put large, heavy objects on lower shelves and securely fasten shelves to walls. Brace or anchor high or top-heavy objects. When building or remodeling, always follow codes to minimize earthquake hazards.

Keep a flashlight and battery-powered radio in the home, ready for use at all times. Keep family immunizations up to date. Show your family how to turn off electricity, gas, and water at main switches and valves. Hold occasional home earthquake drills so your family knows how to avoid injury and how to remain levelheaded during an earthquake. Also have responsible family members receive first aid instruction because medical facilities may be overloaded immediately following a severe earthquake (check with your local Red Cross for training seminars).

Special advice: During an earthquake, try to remain calm, reassure others and think through the consequences of any action. If indoors, watch for falling plaster, bricks, light fixtures, and other objects such as high bookcases, cabinets, and shelves or other furniture that might slide or topple. Stay away from windows, mirrors, and chimneys. If in danger, crawl under a table, desk, or bed; move to a corner away from windows; or stand in a strong doorway.

Usually it is best not to run outside. However, when outside, avoid high buildings, walls, power poles, and other objects that could fall. Don't run through the streets. If possible, move to an open area away from hazards. If you are in a car, stop in the safest place available, preferably an open area.

Helpful hint: If an earthquake strikes while you are in a high-rise building, get under a desk. Don't dash for exits because stairways may be broken and jammed with people, and power for elevators may fail. In crowded stores, don't rush for a doorway since hundreds of others may have the same idea. If you must leave, choose your exit carefully.

• • •

17 Home Suffers Earthquake

Problem: Home has suffered stress and damage from earthquake.

Background: For what to do during an earthquake, see entry 16. After an earthquake has struck, be prepared for additional earthquake shocks called "aftershocks." Though most of these are smaller than the main shock, some may be large enough to cause additional damage. Respond to requests for help from police, fire fighting, civil defense, and relief organizations, but do not go into damaged areas unless your help has been requested. Don't go sightseeing, especially in beach and waterfront areas where seismic sea waves may strike. Keep the streets clear for emergency vehicles. Cooperate fully with public safety officials. (In some areas you may be arrested for getting in the way of disaster operations.)

What to do: Check your family, those around you, and others in your neighborhood for injuries. Don't attempt to move seriously injured people unless they are in immediate danger of further injury. Don't use your phone except for genuine emergency calls. Use a radio for damage reports and information. Don't share rumors or unverified stories; they often do great harm after disasters. Wear shoes, if possible, in all areas near debris or broken glass. Check for fires or fire hazards. Avoid downed power lines or objects touched by downed wires. Do not enter the home or neighborhood until approved by the authorities.

Special advice: When re-entering the neighborhood or home, check for damage to utility lines and appliances. Do not use matches, lighters, or open-flame appliances until you are sure that there are no gas leaks. Don't operate electrical switches or appliances if gas leaks are suspected. If gas leaks exist, shut off the main gas valve. If there is damage to home wiring, shut off the electrical power. Report damage to the utility companies and follow their instructions. Approach chimneys with caution, first checking them from a distance. Check entire chimney lengths for cracks and damage, particularly in the attic and at the roof line. Unnoticed damage could lead to a fire. Check closets and storage shelf areas. Open closet and cupboard doors carefully and watch for falling objects. Check to see that sewage lines are intact before flushing toilets. Clean up spilled medicines, drugs, and other potentially harmful materials.

Helpful hint: Check your freezer and plan to use foods that will spoil quickly if the power is shut off. Don't eat or drink anything from open containers near shattered glass. If the water is off, you can get emergency water from water heaters, toilet tanks, melted ice cubes, and canned vegetables.

HOME ENVIRONMENT

● ● ● ● ● ● ● ● ● ● ● ● ●

18 Excessive Moisture in Home

Problem: Excess humidity causes condensation that leads to dripping on windows, wet sills, damp walls, mold, wet insulation, wood rot, and metal corrosion.

Background: Humidity is water vapor absorbed in air. Condensation forms when vapor cools enough to convert to liquid, such as the fog, water, or ice seen on a cold window, or the dampness on cold wall surfaces. Excessive humidity can come from sources such as humidifiers, bathing, washing and drying clothes, cooking, washing dishes, mopping floors, plants, pets, plumbing leaks, humans, whirlpools, steambaths, saunas, and attached greenhouses and aquariums. Sources also may include moisture migrating through foundations, brought inside by air leaks, from

combustion venting failure, or from building materials and furnishings.

What to do: A 30% to 50% humidity level is enough to control dry skin problems, dry throats, coughing, and static electricity. Higher levels may increase potential for mold and mildew. Even reasonable indoor humidity, however, can cause condensation and wet insulation in cold climates if water vapor penetrates into cool parts of the home, such as attics. (Holes where wires, pipes, ducts, or light fixtures enter attics should be sealed to prevent humid

air from entering.) Wood rot may occur in studs, wall sheathing, or roof decking if condensation is prolonged.

Solutions include using bathroom and kitchen exhaust fans or whole house ventilating systems, and controlling excessive moisture sources, such as wet basements, unvented clothes dryers or kerosene heaters, indoor firewood storage, overly frequent showers, or misuse of humidifiers. Installing an interior-side vapor retarder and a continuous air barrier system to keep vapor-laden air from penetrating into cool areas, are helpful as well as installing adequate corner insulation and thermally insulated windows and doors. In bathrooms, using triple-insulated glass, and well-insulated walls and ceilings installed with vapor retarders, can reduce condensation.

Special advice: Excessive condensation can also be caused by having improper vents for fuel-burning equipment, such as furnaces, water heaters, wood-burning stoves, and fireplaces. *If this is the case, take action immediately because this situation can be dangerous.* (See entries for individual appliances and also entries 7 and 8.) To be properly vented, the appliance area should be kept at neutral air pressure with a constant supply of outside air. All exhaust fans, exhaust hoods, and appliance exhausts should be balanced with an adequate supply of outside air brought into the house or directly to the equipment.

Helpful hint: New houses often have a higher indoor humidity the first few years due to the moisture in building materials. Opening windows or extra use of ventilation fans on warm days may help. If moisture problems occur when an automatic set-back thermostat (automatically adjusts the system to save energy) is used, adding a timer to operate the furnace fan several times an hour, or leaving the heat on during the night, may solve the problem.

● ● ●

19 Air Pollution in Home

Problem: Indoor air contains pollutants that have the potential to affect your health.

Background: Although pollutants such as radon (see entry 20) may come from outside air or soil, many indoor air pollutants are generated within the home—sometimes in excess of ten times the concentration of outdoor levels. Besides radon, potential pollutants include asbestos, formaldehyde, nitrogen dioxide, carbon dioxide, and carbon monoxide (see entry 8). Typical sources of asbestos include pipe and duct insulation, shingles, and firewalls. Carbon dioxide sources include unvented combustion and human respiration.

Carbon monoxide and nitrogen dioxide can come from gas stoves, furnaces, cigarettes, woodburning stoves, fireplaces, and unvented space heaters. Formaldehyde can be emitted from newly installed urea-formaldehyde foam insulation, or from new manufactured wood products such as furniture, plywood, particle board, or paneling.

What to do: Ways of measuring indoor air pollution have been developed, but in many cases they involve expensive equipment and technical expertise. Some private laboratories can pinpoint pollutants, but may charge between $300 and $2,000 to do such tests. Relatively inexpensive monitors that measure radon, formaldehyde, and nitrogen dioxide can be installed in your home and later sent to a lab for analysis. The more air exchanges there are within the home the more often indoor pollutants are diluted with outdoor air to lower pollution concentrations. The more tightly concentrated a home, the lower its air-change rate will be. However, proper distribution of outside air within the home must also be considered because indoor pollution is generated in different areas of the home.

Eliminate obvious sources of pollutants, such as all unvented combustion appliances, from the living space. A yellow flame in your gas furnace may indicate insufficient air supply for combustion, causing an increase in carbon monoxide and nitrogen dioxide. Attaching a combustion air duct from the outside to the appliance helps ensure safe combustion and minimizes the use of heated air inside the home. If the home seems too humid or has excessive condensation on windows, remove as many sources of moisture in the house as possible (see entry 18). This may include firewood stored in the basement, clothes hung inside to dry, and leaking basements.

Special advice: High levels of carbon dioxide (CO_2) may indicate that ventilation systems are not delivering enough fresh air. Symptoms may include stuffy air, drowsiness, dizziness, and headaches. First try running several fans at night to help mix air, leaving bedroom doors open and setting fans to blow air out into the hall and living areas. If you have a forced-air heating system, set the furnace fan to run continuously at night. If you don't feel more refreshed in a week or two, try running the fans, plus leaving a window in each bedroom open about a quarter of an inch. Also make sure there is an adequate gap between all interior doors and the floor.

Helpful hint: If the above measures don't help, consider having a mechanical ventilation system installed by a contractor. To determine if a gas furnace is leaking combustion by-products, hire a qualified professional. If you ever smell leaking gas in the home, contact your gas utility company immediately and follow their instructions (also see entry 5).

● ● ●

20 Radon in Home

Problem: Radon gas is present in amounts large enough to cause potential health problems.

Background: Radon is a colorless, odorless, tasteless radioactive gas that is present naturally in the environment. Radon is produced from the radioactive decay of uranium. Very small amounts of uranium and radium are present in almost all rocks and soil, so radon is constantly being produced almost everywhere. Exposure to radon and its decay products can cause lung cancer; the greater the amount and the longer the exposure, the greater the risk. For information on other indoor air pollutants, see entry 19.

What to do: Like all gases, radon moves from high to low pressure by airflow, and from high to low concentrations by diffusion, or mixing. If a building provides an easier route, radon gas may enter, become trapped, and eventually decay. (Underground water and some building materials can also emit radon.) Radon can enter a home through sewer pipes, sump pump openings, cracks in the basement floor and walls, and private wells. A drop in air pressure inside a house can help pull the radon indoors from the surrounding soil. This pressure drop can be created by some mechanical systems, furnace operation, or the use of combustion devices.

Most efforts to reduce radon risks in homes center on reducing the entry of radon gas. (Air-cleaning devices may actually increase the problem.) You can buy relatively inexpensive canister or alpha-track detectors to test for radon in homes. The canisters with activated charcoal are exposed for 48 hours in a closed home and sent to a lab. Alpha-track detectors have a plastic disc which is struck by alpha particles given off by radon decay. The disc, exposed in the home for a period of up to a year, is then read by a lab.

Special advice: High radon levels vary by area within the United States. Alpha-track detectors, which measure long-term averages, are of more value because health risk is related to long-term exposure. When using charcoal canisters, follow directions and keep away from areas of high temperature, humidity, or drafts.

Helpful hint: Professionals in your area also may have more expensive direct-reading instruments to detect radon in your home. They may be set for average results, or to "sniff" out sources of radon entry, and offer immediate readings.

● ● ●

21 | Excessive Lead Around Home

Problem: Lead exposure in home is high enough to threaten health of occupants.

Background: Lead poisoning occurs when too much lead builds up in the body. It can cause learning, behavior, and health problems in children and high blood pressure, and damage to kidneys and reproductive organs in adults. Often there are no symptoms until health problems are very serious, but they can include loss of appetite, irritability, constipation, loss of recently acquired skills, headache, stomach cramps, drowsiness, lack of energy and disrupted sleep patterns.

Sources of lead include cracking, chipping, and peeling lead-based paint, dust from paint chips, soil next to buildings with chipped paint or near homes that have been remodeled or torn down, areas near heavy traffic, or water if the home water system has lead pipes or copper pipes joined with lead solder. Most at risk are children 6 years old and younger who are living in homes built before 1960. Persons remodeling homes also may be at risk if paint has lead in it. (The amount of lead used in household paint was not limited until 1978.) A simple blood test at a local public health clinic or family doctor can determine whether there is too much lead in the body.

What to do: Your local health department can tell you how to have the paint in your home tested for lead. Lead-based paint may have been used on cribs, highchairs, windows, woodwork, walls, doors, railings, and ceilings. Don't let children eat or chew on anything that may have paint on it; check for teeth marks on woodwork. Clean windows often with soap and water because loose paint and dust can build up in window areas. The best solution is to remove the lead source; painting over chipping or peeling lead-based paint does not make it safe. (If you can't remove peeling or chipping lead-based paint right away, block off areas, cover with masking tape, or move cribs or beds away from the wall.)

Since dust can be contaminated, keep the home as dust-free as possible, using a trisodium phosphate detergent to wet mop floors and wipe furniture and windowsills. Wash children's hands before eating, naps, and bedtime; wash bottles, teething rings, and toys often. Keep windows closed on windy days to keep dust out. Don't let children eat outside on the ground, eat dirt, or play right next to the home or the street. Take shoes off before entering the home to avoid tracking dust inside. Wash fruits and vegetables before eating (remove outer leaves of leafy vegetables), and don't store juices or food in open cans. Plant gardens away from the house. Don't use home remedies that contain lead; use non-aspirin pain relievers instead.

Plumbing installed before 1930 may contain lead pipes; homes built before the 1980s may have water pipes joined with lead-based solder. Have your water tested by a certified lab. If you suspect lead is in your water, let it run for a couple of minutes, or until there is a temperature change, each time it has been sitting in the pipes for 6 hours or more. Don't cook, drink, or make baby formula with water from the hot water faucet; hot water dissolves more lead than cold water. If you need hot water, take it from the cold water faucet and heat it.

Special advice: Removing lead-based paint incorrectly can cause a serious health threat. It should be done by a qualified contractor (check with your local health department) who knows safe removal methods, how to contain lead-contaminated debris, and the proper cleanup and disposal of the debris. Special protective clothing and respirators must be worn. Vacuum cleaners with "high efficiency particulate air (HEPA)" filters should be used to clean up dust and debris, areas need to be washed with a trisodium phosphate detergent, then re-vacuumed with the HEPA vacuum a second time. Young children, pregnant or breastfeeding women, and pets should not be allowed in the home while the cleanup is being done.

Helpful hint: Adults who work in jobs that require the use of lead, including painters, remodelers, or workers in smelters or battery plants, should shower and change clothes before coming home.

HOME ELECTRICAL

●●●●●●●●●●●●●

22 Home Wiring Inadequate

Problem: Excess demand on electrical system, which shows up as blown fuses, tripped circuit breakers, dim or flickering lights, or appliances that operate at only partial capacity.

Background: Electrical requirements for the average home have almost tripled since 1955. In 1940, for example, the average home used 30 electrical appliances while today's home uses about 80. The electrical systems of about 90% of homes in the United States are not designed to accommodate the number of appliances currently available. Many homes over 20 years old require complete rewiring, and even a number of newer homes need either rewiring or expanded wiring systems (including new circuits) to handle major appliances.

What to do: If your home's wiring system has any of the symptoms listed below, the individual circuits may be overloaded or the wiring of these circuits may be inadequate. Also see entries 23, 24, and 25 or call a qualified electrician.

- Blown fuses or tripped circuit breakers: When fuses blow and circuit breakers trip frequently, it indicates an overloaded circuit, or that the power drain from appliances is greater than the circuit can handle. Short circuiting in appliances or wiring could also be the problem.
- Lights dim or flicker: This problem can be caused by having too many appliances on one circuit, or by putting too large of a power drain on the circuit when specific appliances are turned on. (It may also be caused by electrical storms or by voltage drops at the power plant.)
- Appliances with heating coils warm up slowly: Inadequate wiring may be indicated by electric space heaters and hot plates

that are slow to warm up, and by similar appliances that require high power and seem to be operating on decreased power.

- Television picture shrinks: If the image on your TV is smaller than the picture tube area, the circuit could be overloaded with too many appliances or extension cords. If it occurs only occasionally, it is probably caused by the heavy current drain of appliances that are started up on the same circuit.
- Air conditioners work at less than full capacity: The heavy power needs of air-conditioner compressors can require more line voltage than circuits provide. With large air-conditioning units, separate circuits may be needed.

Special advice: When in doubt about any electrical wiring problem, consult an electrician. Always use caution when working with electricity. Before proceeding with any electrical work, make sure the main disconnect on the service entrance panel is in the "off" position, or pull the main fuses if the panel is the cartridge fuse type. When working on individual receptacles or light switches, also turn off the circuit breaker for the circuit you will be working on, and test the receptacle with a test light before handling bare wires.

Helpful hint: Never stand on a wet or damp floor when working at the

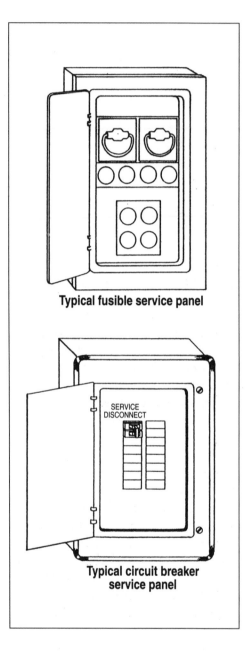

Typical fusible service panel

Typical circuit breaker service panel

SERVICE DISCONNECT

service panel. Wear rubber gloves and stand on a rubber mat for added safety.

●●●

23 Electrical Circuit Fails

Problem: Fuses blow or circuit breakers trip because of problems at the main panel.

Background: Circuit breakers and fuses act as the first line of defense when an electrical failure occurs. When a fuse blows or a circuit breaker trips, it indicates that something is wrong within the circuit. Replacing the fuse or resetting the circuit breaker should not be done until the cause is determined. Ignoring this condition could cause a fire hazard, draw excessive power and run up your electric bill, or make appliances run below optimum levels, which could possibly damage motors and compressors.

What to do: Check entry 24 for problems caused by short circuits, and entry 25 for problems caused by overloaded circuits. Check below for circuit failures that are caused at the main panel. *Do not work on a fused or breaker panel unless you are familiar with electrical safety procedures and are confident of your abilities.*

• Loose connection in a fused panel: After turning off the power, remove the fuses. (Warning: The connections where the main wires enter the panel are *hot*.) A loose screw may be found in one of the fuse sockets. If the bottom of the fuse is blackened, discolored, or pitted, a loose connection may be at fault.

• Loose connection in a circuit breaker panel: After turning power off, remove cover from panel. Inspect the panel for darkened or pitted marks on the bus (the strip of metal where a number of connections are made on the panel) or circuit breakers. Also check the wires connected to the circuit breakers for signs of excessive heat.

• Fuse poorly seated: Although the fuse window shows no indication of burn out, and the bottom is not pitted or discolored, the fuse may not be making contact with the bottom of the receptacle. Remove the fuse and replace it with one of adequate length to make contact.

Special advice: If any of the above conditions exist, contact an electrician. If there is an unused branch space in the existing panel, it may be possible to move the branch wire from the damaged fuse or circuit breaker to the unused space and install a new fuse or circuit breaker. If there are no unused spaces, the entire panel may need to be replaced. If so, consider having the electrician install a larger service to meet future electrical needs more adequately.

Helpful hint: To avoid overloaded circuits, never insert a fuse in a panel that has a higher amperage rating than the rating on the wire for the circuit. Never use a penny or tin foil in a service panel instead of a fuse.

• • •

24 Home Wiring Short Circuits

Problem: Power to a circuit is cut off by a fuse or circuit breaker in the main panel.

Background: If a fuse is blown, the fuse window will appear discolored and the metal strip running across the inside of the window will be broken. This indicates a short circuit caused by either 2 bare wires touching, or by a hot wire grounding out to a metal object somewhere in the circuit. Circuits protected by cartridge fuses will give no visible indication that a short circuit has taken place. Tripped circuits protected by circuit breakers can be identified when the handle of the circuit breaker is in the "tripped" or "off" position.

What to do: If the circuit power cuts off and no fuse appears to be blown, see entries 22 and 23. The method for identifying the cause of a short circuit is the same for fuses or circuit breakers. Disconnect all lights and appliances on the circuit with the blown fuse or tripped circuit breaker. Then replace the blown fuse or turn on the tripped circuit breaker. If the fuse blows or the circuit breaker trips with all appliances unplugged from the circuit, the short is in the circuit wiring itself and the wiring must be repaired or replaced. If the circuit is good, reconnect each light and appliance on that circuit, one at a time.

Special advice: Use extreme caution when reconnecting lights and appliances. Do not connect suspiciously frayed cords to outlets. When you turn on the faulty light or appliance, the fuse will blow or the breaker will trip again. Carefully check appliances for bare cords, broken light sockets, or damaged plugs before replugging.

Helpful hint: If one particular fuse blows several times, shut off all wall switches and appliances on that circuit, and remove all line cords from the sockets. Remove the fuse and screw a 100-watt light bulb into the fuse receptacle. If the bulb lights with all appliances unplugged from the circuit, a short exists within the circuit. If it doesn't light, connect each of the appliances, lamps, and line cords one at a time. If the bulb lights at the fuse panel and the appliance fails to work, you've located the short. Remove the bulb from the panel before disconnecting the faulty appliance.

• • •

25 Circuit Wiring Overloads

Problem: Power to a circuit is cut off because of either temporary overloads or constant overloads.

Background: Most circuit failures are caused by overloads. Electricity in home wiring flows under pressure, much like water moves under pressure in a plumbing system. The electrical pressure is known as voltage. The flow of electricity is called amperage. Wire of a specific size may have too great a resistance to handle the current required of it. If a fuse blows and the window remains clear, an overloaded circuit is most likely the cause. Cartridge-type fuses will give no visible indication of an overloaded circuit. Circuit breakers will be in the "tripped" or "off" position.

What to do: If a circuit fails repeatedly, there may be a short in it (see entry 24) or there may be too many heavy appliances on that circuit. If removing some of the appliances from the circuit does not eliminate the overload, an individual circuit must be added for the appliance with the heaviest current drain. Fused circuits can be corrected to handle temporary overloads by using a time delay fuse of either 15 or 20 amperage. This type of fuse will handle temporary power drains from the start-up of appliance motors. Many electric motors need nearly three times the normal line current for initial starting. Circuit breakers are designed to automatically handle temporary overloads.

Special advice: To check loads on a specific circuit, total the number of watts used for appliances and lights on that circuit at the same time. Appliance wattage rates are usually on the nameplate at the back of an appliance, or on the motor. After adding up the total, divide the sum by 120 volts to calculate the amperages. For example, if the total exceeds 1,800 watts for a circuit with a 15-amperage fuse, or exceeds 2,400 watts for a circuit with a 20-amperage fuse, the circuit is overloaded. One or more appliances may be plugged into another circuit to avoid an overload, as long as new overloads are not created. If overloads remain, call an electrician to add an additional circuit.

Helpful hint: When calculating circuit loads, you may find appliance plates give amperages rather than watts. To convert into watts, multiply amperages by voltage (120 or 240). If horsepower is given on motors, multiply horsepower by 746 to find watts.

•••

26 Electrical Plug Defective

Problem: Plug sparks when used, does not carry power to lamp or appliance, or causes short circuits.

Background: There are eight or more different kinds of receptacle plug configurations, but they all fall within two major categories: flat wire plugs and round cord plugs. Replacement plugs are readily available for both kinds and may be found in two basic types: replacement plugs, which use screws to connect cord wires to the terminals, and quick-connect plugs, which have spikes inside that make contact with the wires. Plugs should be replaced whenever the casing is cracked or damaged, the prongs have become loose or badly bent, the insulation faceplate is gone, or the cord near the plug has become damaged.

What to do: Clip off the old plug and take it with you when buying a replacement. When using a quick-connect flat wire replacement plug, read the general directions below, then proceed by following the manufacturer's instructions, if any are given. For replacing the appliance-end plug, or appliance cord, see entry 27.

- Flat wire plugs: With take-apart replacement plugs, the casing

has a screw which allows the casing to be taken apart in two halves, freeing each prong which has a screw terminal. Remove about ½-inch of insulation from the wires, twist them and hook each wire around a terminal and tighten. Reassemble the casing and install the insulation cover.

Procedures vary in attaching a quick-connect replacement plug because there are at least three different kinds. One kind has a levered clamp at the back which is pulled up, the wire (slitted ¼ inch between strands) is pushed into a hole at the side, and the clamp is pushed back into the casing. With a second kind, the prongs are squeezed together so that the interior can be pulled out. The prongs are spread; the wire inserted, the prongs are closed, and the interior part is pushed back into the casing. A third kind has a wrap-around casing which slips off, then the wire is simply inserted and the casing is slipped back on.

- Round cord plugs: These will have screws to attach wires. Cut

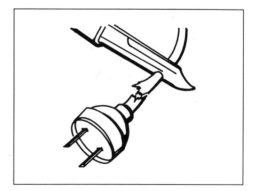

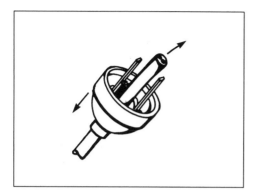

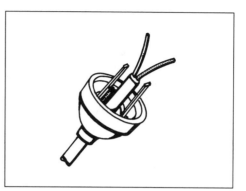

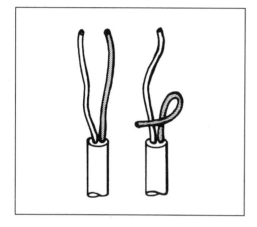

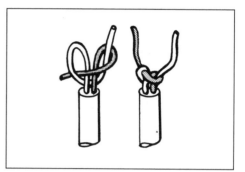

the damaged part of the cord off, then slip the plug onto the cord. Clip and separate the cord and tie what is called an underwriter's knot (see illustration) and pull knot back into plug snugly. Remove ½ inch of the insulation from the ends of the wires, and twist the strands of each wire together clockwise. Wrap the end of the black wire around under the brass screw, wrap the end of the white wire around under the silver screw (insulation should not come under the screws), and tighten screws.

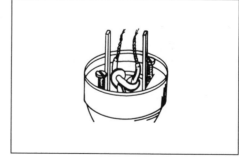

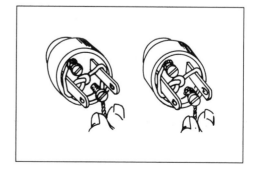

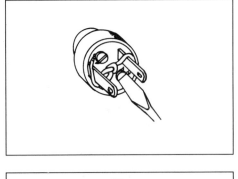

the cord will cause unnecessary wear and premature failure of the plug.

Helpful hint: A wire stripping tool is a low-cost, pliers-like device which makes stripping insulation from wires more precise. Most have holes to accommodate wires in a range from 20- to 10-gauge. You simply select the proper hole, position the wire where you want the insulation to end, then squeeze the handles and pull. It is a worthwhile investment.

• • •

If the cord has solid wires, pre-bend the ends clockwise with needle-nose pliers to fit under screw terminals. On a 3-prong plug there will be a third green wire which is attached to the ground screw terminal. Placing the insulation cover back on plug, and tightening any cord clamp, completes the replacement.

Special advice: Plug prongs sometimes don't fit the receptacle properly. If not, try spreading the prongs of the plug to fit tighter into the receptacle. (Also see entry 28.) To prevent damage to electrical plugs, make it a habit to always remove a plug from a receptacle by grasping the plug, not the cord. Pulling only

27 Appliance Plug or Cord Defective

Problem: The detachable plug, which inserts into an appliance such as a roaster or waffle iron, becomes defective or a small appliance cord becomes frayed or damaged.

Background: Appliance plugs used on small heating appliances are commonly found in three sizes, and may or may not have a control. The cords usually have 2 insulated wires covered by an asbestos protector and a braided cover. Heavy-duty, rubber-covered cords are often used for vacuum cleaners and washing machines and may contain either 2 or 3 wires.

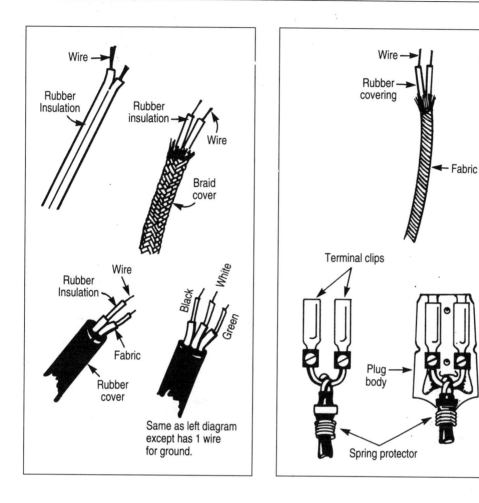

What to do: For replacing the receptacle plug, see entry 26. To replace the plug end, which fits into the appliance, disconnect the cord and the receptacle and disassemble the plug on the end of the cord that connects to the appliance. Keep track of the placement of each part.

Remove 2½ inches of outer covering on the cord, and run the cord end through the plug's spring protector. Temporarily fit the wires into 1 of the 2 plug casing halves to determine where to cut the individual wires so they are of proper length. Then remove ½ inch of the rubber insulation from the end of each wire and tie an underwriter's knot (see entry 26). Pull the cord back snugly against the spring protector and attach wires to terminals on the clips. Place terminal clips and spring into 1 of the plug casing halves and fit the other half over it, replacing the screws or clamps that hold the casing together. Inspect receptacle plug at the other end of cord, and replace it if necessary.

Special advice: Splicing of broken wires within a cord is not recommended, and *any cords spliced on a temporary basis should be replaced as soon as possible.* Splicing for emergency use can be done by cutting out the broken piece and inserting a cord connector. Or an emergency splice can be done by cutting out the broken section, stripping 1 inch of insulation from the wires, twisting them together, and wrapping tape around each wire, then around both wires, and then overlapping the tape onto the cord. *Note: Never splice house wiring even on a temporary basis.* When replacing cords, buy replacements that match the original in wire size and type.

Helpful hint: Always turn any control to "off" and disconnect an appliance cord first from the wall outlet rather than from the appliance. Avoid grabbing the cord to disconnect; grasp the plug instead. Keep oil and grease away from appliance cords, do not place cords under rugs or in doorjambs, avoid sharp bends, and store in a cool and dry place.

● ● ●

28 Outlet Receptacle Defective

Problem: Outlet won't work, sparks, does not receive prongs on plug, or does not grip plugs.

Background: Most homeowners should not have any problem replacing a common-wall electrical receptacle (sometimes called a "duplex" receptacle) if safety precautions are taken and the new receptacle is the same as the one replaced. The receptacle may also be the 3-hole type installed where heavy appliances and tools are used, a protected outlet with a spring-loaded cover that springs back over the openings, or it may be a receptacle-switch combi-

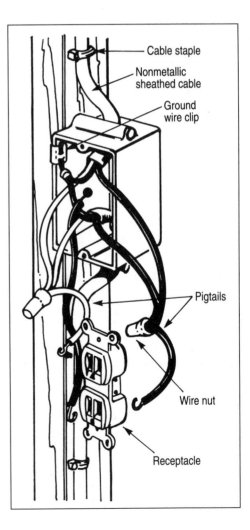

Cable staple

Nonmetallic sheathed cable

Ground wire clip

Pigtails

Wire nut

Receptacle

nation. Older receptacles with 2 slots can be updated to 3-prong types if grounding can be provided; if not, call an electrician for advice.

What to do: The procedure of replacing a receptacle is similar to that of replacing a light switch (see entry 29). *Make certain the power is off,* then remove the cover plate. Pull the old receptacle out and note the position of the wires. Unscrew the terminals so the wires can be removed, then install in the same way on the new receptacle. Hook the wire loops so

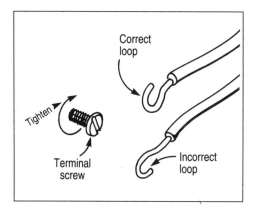

they are clockwise under the terminals on the new receptacle. Reinstall the receptacle in the electrical box, turn on the power and test to see if it is working.

Special advice: Newer polarized outlets have one wide slot and one narrow slot to accept the wide and narrow slots of polarized plugs. The National Electrical Code requires home wiring to be identifiable by color code. Neutral wires are white; live wires are colored, usually black.

Polarized outlets and plugs continue this identification, assuring that the live wire is connected to the incoming side of the switch in an appliance. The wide slot is connected to the neutral (white) wire in the system. In polarized lamp and appliance leads and extension cords, the neutral (white) wire may be ribbed for identification. Non-polarized, 2-wire plugs can be used with a polarized outlet, though the polarization continuity will not be assured.

Helpful hint: Note that all grounding (3-wire) plugs are polarized since the position of the prongs is determined by the third prong. To double-check a new receptacle, you can buy an inexpensive circuit tester. It will indicate if ground, neutral, or hot wires are properly connected, and whether the hot and ground wires are reversed, or whether the hot and neutral wires are reversed. They are usually available where electrical parts are sold.

•••

29 Light Switch Defective

Problem: Switch does not work, works occasionally, or must be repeatedly switched off and on to make light come on.

Background: Correcting a defective light switch is relatively easy, but

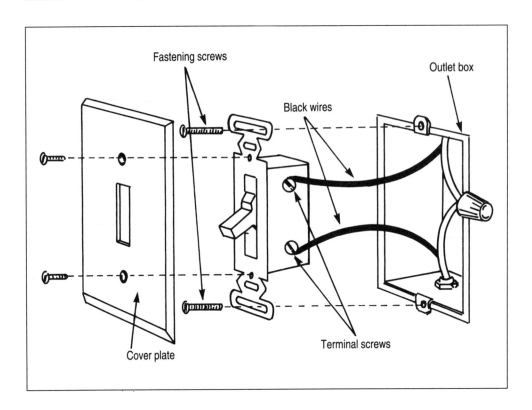

Fastening screws

Outlet box

Black wires

Cover plate

Terminal screws

take proper precautions to avoid electrical shock; *make sure the power is off before working on switch.* Generally, all you need is a screwdriver and pliers. Though light switches can be wired in a circuit in a number of ways, if you buy the identical switch and wire it exactly the same way as the old switch was wired, you shouldn't have any problems. Light switches are sometimes replaced when the problem is a burned-out bulb. Even if you have a switch that controls a number of lamps or fixtures, be sure that the bulbs are working before assuming that the switch is defective.

First replace a bulb in a lamp controlled by the switch with one

you know works, then work the switch. If the bulb doesn't light, try to determine if power is reaching the switch. Check the fuse or circuit breaker in the main panel box that feeds the circuit. Replace the fuse or circuit breaker with one you know works, then try the switch again. If it still doesn't light the bulb, the switch is probably defective.

What to do: To replace a switch, first turn off the power by unscrewing the fuse (or switching off the circuit breaker) or by throwing the main switch to the "off" position. *If you are not sure that the power is off, don't proceed any further until you can get qualified help.* With the power off, remove the switch cover plate. Inside you'll see 2 additional screws that hold the switch mechanism inside the outlet box. By removing these screws you'll be able to pull the old switch out of the box with the electrical wires still attached. Make note of the color and position of the wires and the screws on the switch.

Double-check to be sure you have the same kind of switch and also note the ground wire (usually green), which may run from the switch to a terminal inside the outlet box. (The ground wire in systems using the newer Romex cable will be a bare wire coming out of the cable.) Loosen the screws holding the wires to the old switch, remove the switch, and attach the wires in the same way onto the new switch. Fasten the switch inside the outlet box, replace the cover, and restore the power.

Special advice: If the new switch doesn't work, re-check to make sure that the fuse or circuit breaker for that circuit is supplying power. Occasionally a circuit breaker, even a new one, may be defective. Also, though a fuse is of the proper amperage, it may be just slightly shorter than the original, resulting in a power interruption to a particular circuit.

Helpful hint: Hook the loops of the wires under the screw terminals in a clockwise manner so that they remain in position as the screws are tightened. Two-way, single-pole switches will have a screw on each side of the switch. Three-way switches will have three terminals; two will be brass for connecting red and black hot wires, and the third, usually bronze or silver (sometimes black), is for connecting the white neutral wire.

● ● ●

30 Lamp Socket Defective

Problem: The bulb flickers or will not work in a lamp, even though other lamps work using the same receptacle.

Background: Lamp sockets, especially those with switches, are liable to failure, and can be replaced relatively easily. Replacements are available for major types, which include those with twist knobs, push knobs, and pull chains. Often replacements come in blister-packs, with instructions on the back. The parts of a lamp socket include the outer shell with insulating sleeve inside; the socket, which has 2 terminals; and the cap which also has an insulated liner. The outer shell, which holds the socket, clips into the cap by pressure.

What to do: Use proper electrical safety procedures, and make sure lamp is unplugged from receptacle. To replace a socket, first remove the shade and harp (the metal part that holds the shade). Squeeze the outer shell to remove from the cap; it should be marked "press" in an area near its base. Note the position of the wires, then remove wires from screw terminals. (With a newer lamp cord, 1 of the 2 wires may have ridged insulation covering; this wire goes under the silver screw while the other goes under the brass screw.) Fit the new socket inside the outer shell with its insulating sleeve, and lock the unit back into the cap.

Special advice: Before replacing the socket, first look for the other possible problems. Try plugging the lamp into another outlet, and also try a new bulb. If it doesn't work, check the plug and the cord carefully to see that they are in good shape. If they appear to be functional, unplug the lamp and remove the bulb. Scrape the contact with a screwdriver, and pry it up if it appears to be flattened. Insert bulb and try it again. If it still doesn't work, replace the socket.

Helpful hint: If you see that the cord is frayed or damaged, be sure to repair (or preferably replace) it because dangerous shocks may result, especially if you handle the lamp while standing on a wet floor. (See entry 27 for general advice on replacing cords.)

• • •

31 Ground Fault Circuit Interrupter Device Defective

Problem: When the test button is pushed, the device does not trip to indicate that it is working.

Background: A ground fault circuit interrupter, often referred to as a GFCI or a GFI, is designed to interrupt the flow of electricity if a current leakage to ground occurs anywhere in the line. Circuits protected by such a device reduce the danger of current leakage and the possible shock hazard when someone touches an appliance or light fixture that is not properly grounded. The National Electrical Code and most local codes require that bathroom circuits, outdoor and underground wiring, especially swimming pool lighting, be GFCI protected. Several types are available that include GFCI receptacles and GFCI circuit breakers, which combine a ground fault interrupter and circuit breaker in one device.

What to do: When the test button is pushed, a simlated ground fault is introduced into the sensing circuit. A properly installed device will trip and must be reset after the test button is pushed. If the device does not trip, make sure that the circuit is receiving power; the device must be energized to operate, even when testing. If it is receiving power and does not trip when tested, have an electrician check to see that all connections are properly made. If a properly wired and energized GFCI does not trip when tested, it should be replaced immediately because the protection has been lost.

Special advice: Receptacles with built-in ground fault protection are installed similarly to the way standard duplex receptacles are installed. Some models have "pigtails" for connections; others have normal screw connections. Feed-through models provide ground fault protection to other receptacles connected to the same cable "downstream" of the GFCI receptacle.

Helpful hint: Some GFCI receptacles require extra-deep electrical boxes, so check the instruction sheet provided for size before buying and attempting to install. Also note that GFCI circuit breakers are connected in the main panel differently than standard circuit breakers.

● ● ●

32 Doorbell Defective

Problem: The doorbell doesn't ring at all, works only occasionally, or rings continuously.

Background: In most all cases the doorbell will be powered with low voltage, fed from a transformer that converts 120-volt household current to the 6- to 8-volt range for older systems, or to a 12- to 14-volt range for newer systems. The low-voltage power supply wire is interrupted by the push button switch at the door. When the button is pushed, the power is fed through to the bell. Weather can corrode outdoor switch contacts, and vibration can loosen connections at the bell.

What to do: Possible causes for the failure include a faulty switch, wiring, transformer, or the bell itself. Chances are best that the switch may be bad, so start there. Unscrew the push button and check to see that the wires are making good contact under the 2 screws behind the switch. If the connections are good, touch a screwdriver between the 2 screws or remove the 2 wires and touch them together. (Normally low-voltage wiring does not carry enough current to be dangerous *except at the transformer*.) If the doorbell rings, the problem is the push button. Clean its terminals with sandpaper or electrical contact cleaner. If that doesn't work, replace it; replacements are low cost and readily available.

If, when the wires are touched together, the bell doesn't ring but the transformer hums, suspect a wiring defect or the bell itself. If the transformer doesn't hum, suspect defective wiring or a burned-out transformer. Check all wires from the transformer to the push button and back to the bell, making sure connections are good. Inside some bells you may be able to clean the contact breaker points with fine sandpaper or emery cloth. The gong should touch the bell when the contact points are closed; if not, bend the hammer slightly.

Special advice: If the transformer is suspected, *be sure to turn off the master electrical switch before disconnecting* because the wires feeding the transformer will be 120 volts. If you are not positive the transformer is bad, have it tested at an electrical supply dealer before buying a replacement.

Helpful hint: To assure your safety in case the transformer has gone bad and is not reducing power to low voltage, use a tester and touch its leads to the 2 screws on the push button switch. A 120-volt tester will not light up if the transformer is reducing the power to low voltage.

HOME PLUMBING

● ● ● ● ● ● ● ● ● ● ● ● ●

33 Toilet Is Plugged Up

Problem: Toilet becomes clogged and does not flush, or flushes only partially.

Background: Excess material may plug up a toilet, but often nondegradable items, including children's plastic tub toys, combs, and other items that fall into the bowl and clog the trapway, cause stoppages. A toilet that does not flush properly may indicate defective toilet plumbing (see entries 34 and 35) or problems within the drain system beyond the toilet (see entry 46).

What to do: The first method of attack is to use a rubber-cupped plunger, often referred to as a plumber's friend. To make this tool work more effectively, coat the outside lip of its working end with petroleum jelly. Position it in the toilet bowl, making sure the cup part is covered by water. Plunge it vigorously for a few minutes, then pull it

away sharply. Try this several times. If plunging doesn't clear the toilet, a second approach is to use a wire hanger or what is known as a closet or toilet auger, a special plumber's snake composed of a flexible length of cable with a sharp, spiralled hook on one end and a handle on the other.

Use an auger carefully because it can scratch the porcelain. Push the auger into the trap while turning the handle until it bites into the clog. When you think you have dislodged the blockage, try flushing with wet toilet paper in the toilet bowl. If the water goes down, but not the paper, the drain pipe is still obstructed. Try using the auger again. In extreme cases, you may need to have the toilet removed to clear the blockage, or to gain access to the drain pipe below.

Special advice: Do not use commercially available drain cleaners, or bleach solutions in a toilet because noxious gases may be produced if the chemicals mix. Drain cleaners are also ineffective in toilets because the structure of the trap prevents the cleaner from reaching the clog. Also do not use commercially available balloon-type devices which attach to a garden hose; the pressure they exert may break the toilet.

Helpful hint: If you suspect a foreign item is causing the blockage, try holding a small compact-size mirror down in the opening, and shining a flashlight on it to illuminate the passageway. Then try to dislodge the object with a wire or toilet auger.

● ● ●

34 Toilet (Old-Style) Runs

Problem: Mechanisms inside toilet tank allow water to continue to run after toilet is flushed.

Background: To diagnose toilet problems, first lift off the tank cover and watch the mechanisms in action when the toilet is flushed. Next turn off the water supply to the toilet and empty the tank of excess water. Specific repairs will depend on the age and style of the mechanisms inside the toilet. Both older and newer styles have a mechanism to actuate an inlet valve that lets water into the tank, and a mechanism attached to the trip lever that allows water to flow out of the tank. The following tips apply to the old-style components (see entry 35 for troubleshooting toilets with new-style mechanisms and entry 36 for flushing problems).

What to do: On the inlet side, the old-style ball cock mechanism has a valve that opens and closes by a rod that connects to a float ball. As the ball rises in the tank it shuts off incoming water. On the outlet side, older toilets often have a ball-type device which fits into the seat at the bottom of the tank and holds water until the toilet is flushed. This ball is known as a stopper ball, tank ball, or flapper.

If the tank does not refill, first check to see that the stopper ball is in good condition and is seated properly. Adjust its chain or its guide arm, lift wires and the trip lever so that the ball falls straight onto the seat. Scrape away any corrosion from valve seat. If this fails, the easiest way to correct the problem is to replace the stopper ball and valve seat with a new-style rubber flapper assembly.

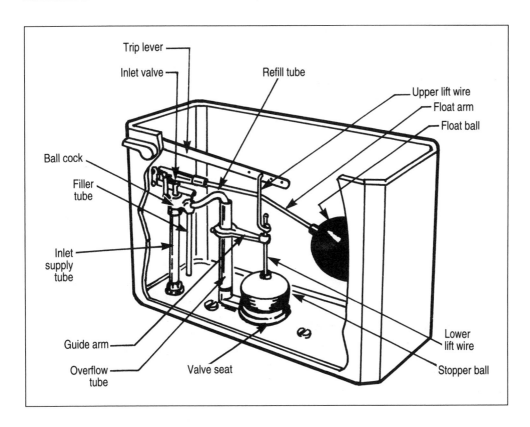

If the stopper ball works, check the float ball and rod assembly next. Make sure the float ball does not touch the tank wall. The float ball may not rise high enough to shut off the inlet valve; if so, check for a leaking float ball, which will prevent it from rising high enough to shut off the water. If the ball leaks, it is easily replaced; just unscrew it from the end of the rod.

If the float ball is set too high, however, it may allow water to flow over and into the overflow tube. In this case, bend the float arm down until it is 1 inch below the top of the tube; this will lower the water level. If the float ball is set right, but water continues to flow, the inlet valve in the ball cock assembly is most likely defective. You can replace the valve washer, the entire inlet valve, or the entire ball cock assembly.

Special advice: In some cases, a running toilet can be caused by a refill tube end that is down too far in the overflow tube, with its end below the water level. The refill tube then becomes a siphon, draining water out of the tank. To correct, reposition the tube so there is space between the end and the water level. Also, when troubleshooting with a running toilet, carefully examine the base of the overflow tube. Corrosion can create holes that allow water to drain continually from the tank.

Helpful hint: Low-cost toilet tank repair kits are readily available for both old- and new-style components. Depending on the problem, instead of replacing major parts of an older system, installing new-style components may be the best bet for long-lasting, trouble-free performance.

•••

35 Toilet (New-Style) Runs

Problem: Water continues to run inside toilet after the flush cycle.

Background: Newer toilets and replacement kits substitute the older ball cock mechanism (see entry 34) with one that uses a floating cup (instead of the rod and float-ball arrangement) to open and close the inlet valve. Newer replacement kits also have a more simple flapper device to hold water in the tank than the old stopper ball with its lifting wires. As with old-style components, continuous running may be caused by a number of conditions, including water draining out of the tank when it shouldn't.

What to do: If a toilet has a new-style inlet valve unit in place of the older ball cock valve assembly, and it turns on and off by itself without

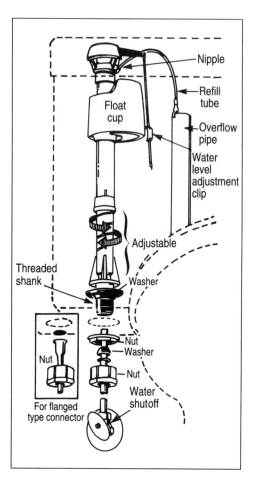

being flushed, the cause may be a faulty tank ball or flapper, or a misdirected refill tube.

Check the tank ball or flapper to see if it is worn, dirty, or misaligned with the flush valve seat. Also check to see if the seat is corroded, preventing the stopper from sealing properly. Clean the tank ball and seat with steel wool; if the leak persists, replace with new-style kit. Next check to make sure that the refill tube from the inlet valve unit is not pushed too far down the overflow pipe. This can result in a siphoning action from the tank to the overflow pipe which lowers the tank water level and causes the inlet valve to turn on. To correct, make sure the refill tube is attached to the top of the overflow tube above the tank water line.

If the inlet valve won't shut off and continues to allow water to enter the tank, the problem can be debris under the inlet valve. Calcium deposits, or particles of corroded pipe, stones, rubber, or solder, can be carried by water to the valve area and become trapped. To fix, shut off the water supply and follow the manufacturer's instructions to remove the unit's upper assembly. Then place an inverted cup over the lower unit and turn the water on and off a few times to flush debris out of the water line. With well systems that constantly circulate such debris, the best solution may be to install a filter.

Special advice: If flushing the water line does not correct the problem, the seal on the inlet valve assembly may be split or cracked. You may be able to buy a replacement seal in stores that sell inlet valve assemblies. If not, contact the manufacturer or replace the entire assembly.

Helpful hint: Some new-style inlet valve assemblies use a float cup to achieve the proper water level. The float cup uses water for ballast. Before adjusting, hold the float cup under water for a few seconds during the fill cycle to allow it to fill

with water. Then adjust for the correct water level.

● ● ●

36 Toilet Flush Inadequate

Problem: Toilet does not flush, provides an inadequate flush, or overflows.

Background: If toilet tank refills, flushing problems are usually caused by the mechanism that allows water to drain into the bowl. Or, in the case of overflows, the problem may be due to blockages in the bowl, outlet, sewer lines or septic tank. For problems caused by the tank mechanism, see the following information. For problems due to blockages in the bowl, see entry 33. For problems within the sewer lines, see entry 46.

What to do: If a toilet with an old-style tank ball only provides partial flushing when the lever is pulled, it is likely that the ball is not lifting high enough from its seat and reseats before the flush is complete. To fix, adjust the upper lift wire so that the tank ball is pulled high enough off of the seat to allow for a complete flush when the lever is pulled. (You may also raise the lift wire guide, which fits around the overflow tube.) Also check the lower lift wire and lever to see that they are operating properly. The lower lift wire should slide easily through the guide arm. If the toilet has a new-style flapper with a chain or strap connected to the trip lever, reduce any slack in the chain.

Special advice: Not enough water in the tank, or a worn-out inlet valve assembly can cause an inadequate flush. If the tank fills only partially, raise the water level by gently bending the float ball rod upward. (Do not raise water lever higher than 1 inch below the top of the overflow tube.) On two-piece toilets (with tanks that are fastened to the bowl), check for leaks where the two join. If leaking, tighten bolts or replace washers on the bolts inside the tank.

Helpful hint: Newer kits for replacing older tank ball assemblies with vinyl flappers and stainless steel replacement drain seats are available. If incorrectly installed, short-length flushes may result. With slanted drain seats, the assembly should be installed so its hinge is not parallel to the overflow tube. If it must be, then check manufacturer's instructions on how to trim stop tabs on the unit to increase the length of the flush.

●●●

37 Toilet Makes Noises

Problem: Toilet makes excessive noise during the flushing cycle.

Background: Toilets that make excessive gurgling or splashing sounds, or that whine or clunk during the flush cycle, likely have defective parts or need adjustment. Most noise problems can be isolated and repaired, regardless of the toilet's age or its components.

What to do: If the inlet valve or ball cock assembly closes with a loud noise (known as a water hammer), it may be because the water pressure is too high. You can try reducing the pressure by partially closing the water supply valve next to the toilet. (Also see entry 43 on water hammer solutions.) However, if the water supply is restricted too much a whining sound may result. Normally keep the water supply valve open as far as possible.

If the toilet still whines, check for corrosion debris at the water supply valve and at the ball cock or inlet valve inside the tank. Worn-out ball cock or inlet valves can also cause excessive noise. Replace washers, if possible, or the entire unit. If the toilet's fill cycle is long or noisy, it may be caused by a partially plugged valve inlet or supply line. Try to clean out the inlet passage of a new-style inlet valve with a knitting needle or a straightened coat hanger.

Special advice: A splashing sound can be caused by the refill tube pointing straight down inside the overflow pipe or spraying water directly into the tank. Either problem can be corrected by repositioning the refill tube so that the water coming out of it hits the inside wall of the overflow pipe.

Helpful hint: When installing or replacing water supply stop valves, ball cock assemblies, or inlet valve units, be sure to clear any debris from the water line before final assembly. (Instructions that come with replacement parts tell how to clear debris from the water line.)

• • •

38 Toilet Base Leaks

Problem: Leak develops at the base of the toilet, between toilet and the toilet flange of the waste pipe.

Background: Occasionally the wax ring between the toilet and waste pipe will lose its seal and allow leakage. New wax rings are available at hardware stores and home centers, however, the toilet must be removed to install the new ring. Before removing, make sure any moisture is not due to tank condensation, or to a leak between the tank and base on a 2-piece toilet.

What to do: Buy a replacement wax ring. Turn off the water at the supply valve near the toilet or at the main water supply valve. Disconnect water supply at the base of the tank. Drain the toilet tank by flushing and remove the remaining water

using sponges or rags. Take the caps and nuts off of the toilet's mounting bolts, and lift the toilet off its mount. Temporarily stuff a rag into the opening in the floor to keep sewer gas from escaping, then clean up the old gasket or setting compound on the floor.

Turn the toilet upside down (being careful to prevent scratches), then remove the old wax ring. Slightly warm the new wax ring and press into position. Turn the toilet right side up and place it into position, allowing the toilet bolts to protrude through the holes in the base. Press down, with your full weight, in a slight twisting motion on the center of the top of the toilet. Replace the washers and nuts and then the caps.

Special advice: The toilet may have been installed with a gasket, not a wax ring. A gasket is formed by the toilet bowl setting compound in the circular recess in the base of the bowl. Simply remove this material before installing the new wax ring.

Helpful hint: If bolts were difficult to turn or were damaged when removed, use new bolts after replacing the wax ring (liquid products that loosen rusted bolts are available at your local hardware store). When replacing the bolts that hold down the toilet base, tighten only until a snug fit is reached. Do not overtighten because you may crack the porcelain base.

• • •

39 Faucet Drips

Problem: Faucet continues to drip and waste water when turned off.

Background: There are several types of faucets found in homes today, including the washer type, the washerless type, the spring-and-valve type, and the disk type. The repair procedure differs for each type. Because replacement parts vary so much, it is best to find a hardware supplier in your area that has replacement part reference books and to work with them to find the parts you need. When possible, try to determine the manufacturer of the unit before you go to the hardware store, and take the old parts along with you for reference. If water is leaking out near the handle, along the stem, see entry 40.

What to do: If a faucet begins to leak, never use excessive force to try to close it because that will only cause damage. Nearly all faucets can be taken apart to replace defective parts. Before beginning to work on a faucet, turn off the stop valves on the hot and cold lines. If you don't have stop valves, you will have to turn off the main water supply valve and work on the faucet when the rest of the home can get by without water (or have a plumber do the work).

With washer-type faucets, dripping water is often caused by worn-

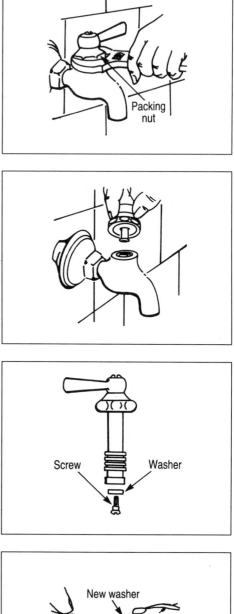

Packing nut

Screw   Washer

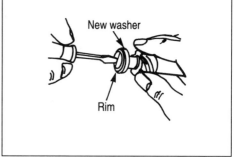

New washer

Rim

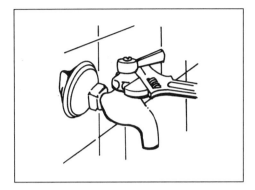

Helpful hint: If there are no stop valves near the fixture where a faucet must be replaced, consider installing new stop valves at the time of the replacement. They will allow you to isolate the fixture and still have water throughout the rest of the house the next time the faucet needs attention.

● ● ●

out washers. Replacement involves taking out the screw in the handle (which may be covered by a decorative cap), taking off the handle, loosening the packing nut, and removing the spindle and washer assembly. A screw holds the washer in place. Replace it with the correct-size washer and reassemble. **Note:** If washers must be replaced often, it may be a sign that the faucet seat is worn. If the seat is replaceable, install a new faucet seat insert, or reseat (smooth the seat with a seat dressing tool). If a worn faucet seat is not removable, the only option is to use this tool. For other types of faucets, consult product sheets, detailed how-to books, or your local parts supplier.

Special advice: If the faucet that drips is more than 5 years old, you may want to consider replacement rather than repair—unless the original is a high-quality faucet. More expensive, quality replacement faucets are generally worth the money; they can last up to three times as long as inexpensive faucets, saving both replacement and labor costs.

40 Faucet Handle Leaks

Problem: Water comes out along the handle of the faucet when it is turned on.

Background: Some faucets, usually old-style units, use either a washer or packing (which looks somewhat like greased yarn) to keep water from escaping along the spindle. In this case, the problem will most likely be with the washer or packing material under the packing nut, not the faucet's washer (see entry 39).

What to do: If water is leaking around the handle area, remove the handle and try to tighten the packing nut. If this doesn't correct the problem, remove the packing nut. If there is a washer under it, replace it. If there is no washer, you will need to unwind the old packing and replace it. After wrapping the spindle with new packing material, replace the packing nut. The packing nut

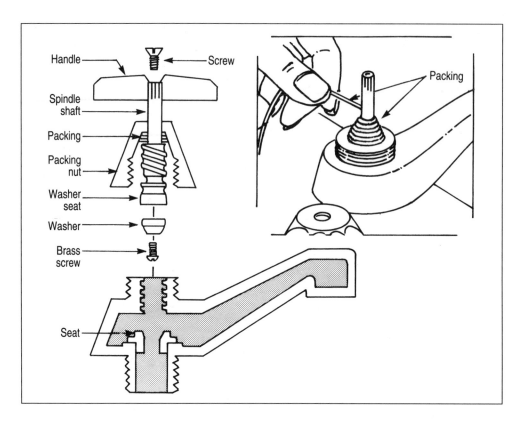

will compress the packing material in place. Replace the handle and turn the water back on at the shutoff valve.

Special advice: Mixing faucets, which are used on sinks, laundry tubs, and bathtubs, consist of 2 separate units, with the same spout, that need to be repaired separately. Most packing nuts may be loosened with an adjustable wrench, and most will loosen by turning counterclockwise. (**Caution:** Avoid using excess pressure with wrenches because it can cause damage and create the need for new parts.)

Helpful hint: When buying packing material, ask your supplier to see any improved versions in stock. Some newer, nylon-coated materials help faucet handles turn easier and last longer than the older packing materials do.

●●●

41 Water Pipe Leaks

Problem: Water drips, leaks, or squirts from the side of a pipe or at pipe joints.

Background: A leaking pipe can occur at any time, especially in older homes. Whenever a leak is detected in a pipe, first turn off the water supply to that area at the nearest valve. Or, if necessary, turn off the water at the main supply valve. (All members of the household should know where the main supply valve is located in case this type of emergency occurs.)

What to do: After the water is turned off, decide whether to call a plumber or to try to fix the problem yourself. For smaller leaks in pipes, hardware stores and home centers carry a variety of clamp-in-place devices, which can be used to seal leaks on pipes at least 1½ inches in diameter. (Applying chewing gum or wrapping with tape with not work because neither gum nor tape can withstand the water pressure in pipes.)

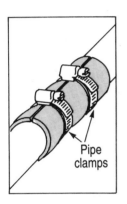

Pipe clamps

You may, however, be able to stop leaking at pipe joints by applying epoxy —at least on a temporary basis. Turn off the water, clean the metal well, and apply the epoxy in a thick layer all around the leaking joint. If

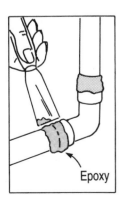

Epoxy

the joint still leaks, the only option may be to replace the fitting. Joint leaks in galvanized, threaded pipe can sometimes be stopped by tightening the threads. But, since this opens up the next set of threads, you have to work back to what is known as a union. Copper, galvanized, or plastic pipe can be repaired by sawing out bad sections and replacing them using special transition fittings.

Special advice: When working with old galvanized steel pipe systems, it's best to always use 2 pipe wrenches. Avoid banging or applying excessive pressure on the pipes because you may cause more joint leaks in the system by doing so. Whenever a pipe leak develops, also inspect the rest of the water supply piping. It may be possible that entire sections should be replaced, especially if water pressure is low (see entry 44); a plumber can offer advice if this is the case.

Helpful hint: If local codes allow, sections of metal pipe may be repaired with plastic pipe and fittings, which are easier to work with than metal. Special transition fittings are used between the old metal and new plastic pipe. Check with home centers or other suppliers of plastic pipe and fittings for supplies.

●●●

42 Water Pipes Are Frozen

Problem: Lack of heat, or unusually cold weather, causes water in pipes to freeze solid.

Background: When water supply pipes become frozen, they should be thawed out promptly to avoid any possible bursting. A bulge may indicate the location of the frozen area in soft copper or lead pipe, but bulges may not be visible in pipes made from other metals. If the pipes involved have split open, they will spray out water if the water is not turned off before it thaws. Sections of bulged or split pipe must be replaced.

What to do: Use some form of heat to melt the ice in the pipes. When thawing water pipes, start on the supply side and keep a faucet in the "on" position so you will know when a flow starts. A good way to defrost frozen pipes is to restore heat to the area. You may also wrap old cloth around pipes and pour boiling water over them. Or you can use a heat lamp, a hair dryer, or electrical heating tape to defrost them. (Avoid using a propane torch because its concentrated heat may create steam that could cause the pipe to burst.) Heat lamps should be kept at least 6 inches away from any walls. Electrical heating tape, covered with insulating tape, can be wrapped around pipes that freeze frequently, and plugged in during extremely cold weather.

Special advice: With waste or sewer pipe, start at the lower end and work upward, if possible, so that the water will be able to flow away as the ice melts. You may be able to thaw frozen traps, waste pipes, drains, and sewer pipes by pouring boiling water into them through the drain opening or trap. If that doesn't work, call a plumber.

Helpful hint: In many cases, pipes near an outside wall tend to freeze because they do not have enough insulation. Wherever pipes become frozen, consider adding insulation to the outside walls in that area. (Opening up a portion of the wall may be necessary to gain access to add the insulation.) If pipes next to an outside wall freeze occasionally, consider keeping the wall open (remove the sheetrock or paneling) at that point and installing a louver so the home's heat will keep the temperature in the outside wall above freezing.

•••

43 Water Pipes Are Noisy

Problem: Pipes make noises whenever water is used or turned off.

Background: Whistling, banging, humming, or chattering sounds coming from plumbing pipes are often fixable. Modern plastic plumbing lines are noisier than older galvanized pipes. However, if water lines hum excessively, the cause may be vibration or blocked piping. Whistling and chattering are often caused by faulty faucet washers or spindles. Loud hammering of pipes can result when faucets are closed, or when the flow of water to the clothes washer or dishwasher is abruptly stopped. Often the solution is installing air chambers in the system, or "recharging" existing air chambers.

What to do: If the pipes produce a humming sound, hold a pipe to see if the humming is caused by vibration. If it is, you may be able to solve the problem by installing padding between the pipe and wall. (If pipes hum because they are old and blocked, replacement may be the only solution.) If the noise results only when one faucet is used, the problem may be a broken or damaged washer or a damaged washer seat. If the noise is a hum or honking when the toilet is used, the problem may be a faulty inlet valve or an inlet valve that is clogged by debris (see entries 34 and 35).

Loud banging that occurs when faucets are shut off quickly is called a water hammer. Check to make sure pipes are securely fastened in the hangers that hold them. If your home does not have air chambers, which provide a cushion of air in the system, a large one can be installed on the main water line or smaller individual chambers can be installed behind each fixture.

Special advice: If your home already has a water chamber in the system, it may be waterlogged (the section of pipe which normally has air in it that acts as a cushion has become filled with water). To correct this, turn off the main water valve and open all the faucets to drain the system. Leave them half way open. Close faucets on the lower floor and turn on the water. As faucets begin to run on lower floor, turn them off and flush any toilets. Do the same on the next floor and third floor. This should automatically replace the water in the air chamber with air.

Helpful hint: Noises, which at first appear to be coming from the plumbing system, may also be caused by splashing in toilet tanks, boilers that have dirty water, or water heaters. Check the tips on water heaters presented in the chapter on home appliances.

• • •

44 Water Pressure Is Low

Problem: The flow of water from faucets and other fixtures is not adequate or is much lower than normal.

Background: If the home's water supply comes from a municipal system, the pressure in the water mains should be sufficient. Inspect the piping system to be sure large enough pipes were initially installed (see Special Advice for correct pipe sizes). In older homes corrosion may build up on the inside, preventing adequate flow. If the pipes in your home are 30 years old or more, built-up corrosion may limit water flow to half of what it should be.

What to do: To test for corrosion buildup inside pipes, open the faucet on your laundry tub and then turn on the faucet farthest away from the water main. If the stream on the second faucet is not at least the width of a pencil, consider replacing the pipes. (Hot water pipes will usually have more corrosion inside than cold water pipes.) A second reason to replace pipe is if you are starting to have problems with leaks within the system (see entry 41). Rust, white, or greenish crusting on pipe or joints may indicate potential leaks.

Special advice: The main distribution pipes generally should have a ¾-inch inside diameter, but branch lines may have a ½-inch inside diameter. Galvanized pipes with a 1⅛-inch outside diameter will have a ¾-inch inside diameter; those with a ⅞-inch outside diameter will have a ½-inch inside diameter. Copper pipes with a ⅞-inch outside diameter will have a ¾-inch inside diameter; those with a ⅝-inch outside diameter will have a ½-inch inside diameter.

Helpful hint: If your home has its own water system and pressure is a problem, check the gauge on the pressure tank. It should read between 40 and 50 pounds. If it reads less than that, the pump may not be operating properly, the pressure may be set too low, or the well system may need attention.

● ● ●

45 Fixture Drain Is Clogged

Problem: Water drains slowly or not at all through plumbing fixture drains.

Background: Assuming that the plumbing for the fixture was correctly installed, most blockages occur close to the fixture's trap—especially if the clog develops quickly and no other fixtures in the house are affected. If a volume of water can be run into the fixture before it backs up, or if other fixtures are affected, the blockage may be further along in the drain system. If the blockage is in the main house drain, it may first show up at bottom-level floor drains. For toilet blockages, see entry 33.

What to do: Drains can be unclogged using several methods, including using a force cup with

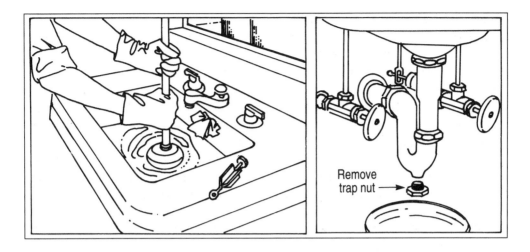

Remove
trap nut →

handle (often called the plumber's friend), by removing the trap to clean it, by using a flexible coil spring auger, or by using chemical drain cleaners. (Note: If the trap below the fixture is accessible, one option is to put a bucket under it, remove the clean-out plug and rid it of debris with a bent coat hanger. If the trap doesn't have a clean-out plug, you'll need to remove the entire trap. Be cautious about collecting waste water, especially if any chemicals have been used.)

If you use a plunger, partly fill the sink or bowl with water and plug the overflow drain. On tubs you will need to remove the pop-up, or trip-lever, drain-stopper mechanism to be able to plug the overflow opening (see entry 47). On double sinks you need to plug the second drain. *Don't use a plunger if chemicals have been used.* Coat the lip of the plunger cup with petroleum jelly and forcibly work it up and down several times. After the pipe is

cleared, pour boiling water through the drain to clear the waste line.

If plunging doesn't work, try using an inexpensive drain-clearing tool available at most hardware stores and home centers. The tool consists of a coil spring cable with a corkscrew-type auger on the working end. An offset, tubelike handle with a thumb setscrew slips over the cable. The cable's auger end is pushed into the drain until the clogged area is reached, then the handle is slid toward the drain, the thumb screw is tightened, and the offset handle is cranked. As progress is made, the screw is loosened and more cable is fed into the drain. (Note: A special version of this drain-clearing tool is sold especially for toilets and is often called a closet auger.)

Special advice: The drain-clearing tool's spiraled auger can be threaded through drains with crossbars. For pop-up drains, you can try to remove the drain plug by turning and lifting. If that doesn't work, loosen the screw and nut on the lift rod under the sink and withdraw the lift rod. If the tool can't be worked through the drain opening, it can be fed through the trap's clean-out plug (if it has one).

Helpful hint: A plunger and a small cable auger should be sufficient for most home uses so if these don't work, consider calling a professional. Try to avoid using liquid drain cleaners when possible because they can damage pipes and drain traps. For blockages beyond the fixture area, see entry 46.

• • •

46 Drain Pipes Are Clogged

Problem: Drain pipes are clogged or drain slowly and clog appears to be beyond fixture.

Background: Blockages further along fixture waste pipes are less common, and require the use of tools, such as a cable auger (sometimes called a plumber's snake), a hydraulic opener, or a flat steel sewer tape. The blockage may be in the waste pipe running from a single fixture, in a branch drain fed by more than one fixture, or in the main house drain. Unless you have the equipment and time, consider calling a professional to unclog these blockages. For blockages near fixtures, see entry 45.

What to do: Flexible cable plumber's snakes can be fed into the waste pipe leading from a fixture, through a vent stack or clean-out plug. Flat sewer snakes are useful when the blockage is too solid to be dislodged by a plumber's snake. Feed a garden hose into the pipe and packing rags in the area where it feeds into a drain, can sometimes work. Using hydraulic drain openers (sometimes called expansion nozzles or blast bags) is another way to clear such drain lines for kitchen sinks, bathtubs, showers, washing machines, and main drains. They connect to a

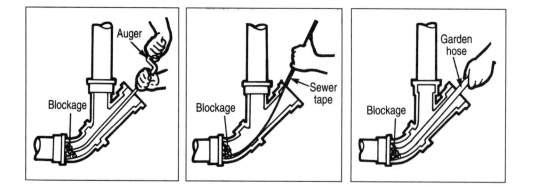

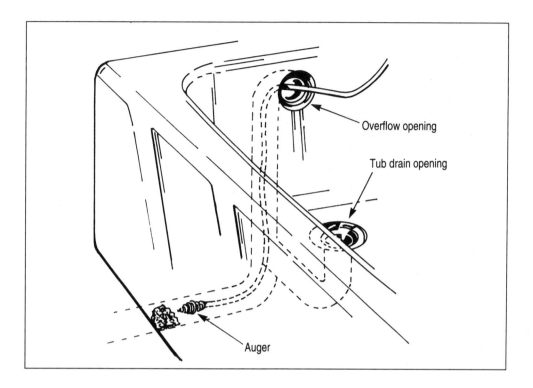

Overflow opening

Tub drain opening

Auger

garden hose and expand inside the drain to form a seal, then pulsate water under pressure to loosen and clear blockages. These units are not intended for toilets, or to be used where chemical drain cleaners are present.

Special advice: Hydraulic openers are sold in various sizes for different pipe sizes. To use in a bathtub, remove the overflow plate and insert at least 10 inches into the overflow pipe. For showers, remove the drain plate and insert the device at least 8 inches into the drain. For kitchen sinks, you must remove the trap from under the sink and insert the opener at least 24 inches into the drain. For washing machine waste lines, the device must be inserted a minimum of 18 inches into the drain. To clean out main drains, insert the unit at least 4 feet into the drain, or further if inserted into the clean-out or roof vent closest to the clogged area. To deflate the unit (so it can be removed from the pipe), turn off the water to the garden hose and loosen the hose coupling at the faucet.

If you have large trees in your yard, the blockage may be caused by tree roots in the sewer line. Root-killing solutions containing copper sulfate can be poured into the drain system, through the main clean-out plug, to remedy the problem. However, the most prudent option may be to hire a professional who uses a root-cutting tool to clear the blockage. Unfortunately, there is no way to be sure that tree roots are blocking sewer lines before choosing to do either one of these expensive procedures.

Helpful hint: Blockages commonly occur in waste lines from clothes washers because discharged lint causes buildups. To prevent inevitable problems, always use a lint trap (either a commercially made device or an old nylon stocking) on the washer discharge pipe.

●●●

47 Bathtub Stopper Defective

Problem: The stopper in the tub doesn't operate, doesn't seal, or causes slow drainage.

Background: Two basic stopper mechanisms are found in tubs. One is the trip-lever type which uses a trip lever to open and close a brass stopper inside the tub's drain. These have a strainer, instead of a stopper, at the drain opening. Another is a pop-up type, in which the lever is linked to the stopper at the drain opening.

What to do: Both types can be taken apart by removing the 2 screws on the decorative overflow plate, lifting the plate off, and then working the mechanism out through the overflow hole. For trip-lever types, clean the mechanism of debris and apply

small amounts of grease on its moving parts. For pop-up types, clean off debris and check the condition of the O-ring, which is positioned underneath the top lip of the stopper. If the O-ring is worn or missing, replace it with a new one. If the pop-up stopper doesn't work even with the new O-ring, remove it and check to see if the linkage needs adjustment. Linkage that is adjusted so that it is too long will keep the stopper from sealing properly.

Special advice: Keep in mind that accumulated hair on the linkage of a pop-up mechanism can cause slow drainage. When adjusting linkage on this type of mechanism, make small adjustments at any one time, by turning the threaded rod into the brass yoke, which connects to the trip lever.

Helpful hint: If the stopper mechanism seems to be unrepairable, or if you only need to replace components, take the entire mechanism when you go to the store so you will be sure to get the right parts.

●●●

48 Showerhead Holes Are Clogged

Problem: Mineral deposits and debris clog up small holes in showerhead.

Background: With use, holes in showerheads can become plugged, causing water to shoot out un-plugged holes with extra force, re-sulting in an uncomfortable shower. Sometimes showerheads become so clogged up that water is released through only a few holes.

What to do: The showerhead may be replaced. However, a good cleaning can restore the device's original per-formance. To unplug a showerhead, remove it, being careful not to scratch its chrome surface by cover-ing it with masking tape, or by using a soft cloth in conjunction with pli-ers or a pipe wrench. Soak the showerhead in a container of vine-gar to loosen the mineral deposits. After soaking, clean out the holes with a toothpick and hot, soapy water, and rinse.

Special advice: Check to make sure that all holes are clear before rein-stalling. On some showerheads you may be able to hold them up to the light to see if all the holes are open.

Helpful hint: If you don't want to, or can't, remove the showerhead, fill a plastic bag with vinegar and tie it over the showerhead to loosen min-eral deposits. Allow to soak over-night and repeat if needed.

● ● ●

49 Well Is Running Dry

Problem: Output from a private well drops below the home's re-quirements.

Background: In rural areas where homes are unable to connect to mu-nicipal water systems, a private well may eventually lose its ability to supply the home with an adequate amount of water. A drop in well per-formance can be caused by a num-ber of factors, including faulty design, poor materials and construc-tion, over-pumping, corrosion, scal-ing, and iron deposits or bacteria. Pumping equipment, instead of the well itself, may also be the cause of the problem.

What to do: Before blaming the well, first check the pumping system for problems. Make sure the pump is supplied with adequate power, that fuses aren't blown, and that the pump itself is not worn out. Many pump failures are caused by corro-sive or incrusting water, as well as power line voltage surges (caused by lightning) that burn out their mo-tors. If all appears to be working, a well contractor in your area may be able to revive the well. Maintenance or rehabilitation is eventually re-quired for most private wells, re-gardless of its location, depth, or type. Many wells no longer supplying adequate water can be restored to produce up to 90% of their original yield.

Special advice: Proper maintenance will reduce the need for well rehabilitation. Ask a well-drilling or groundwater contractor what maintenance should be performed on a regular basis and when the well's output drops below a certain point (usually not less than 50% of the well's original capacity).

Helpful hint: Any noticeable change in water quality may indicate that poor-quality water is entering the well through a hole in its casing. Even if no quality problems are apparent, it's a good idea to have private well water tested regularly. Both private and public water testing facilities are available.

● ● ●

50 Septic System Backs Up

Problem: Wastewater from on-site sewage system backs up into home sewer lines or seeps to the ground surface.

Background: Common problems in private sewer systems are undersized drain fields, undersized septic tanks, and poorly maintained septic tanks (which cause clogged dry-

wells or drainfields). Adequate drainfield size depends on soil type and amount of sewage treated. If the ground above the drain field is especially wet or soggy, or if the capacity of the tank is too small, the system may be inadequate. A 1,000-gallon septic tank is considered a minimum for 3-bedroom homes; 1,250 gallons for 4-bedroom homes, and 1,500 gallons for 5-bedroom homes.

What to do: All septic tanks periodically need to have sludge and scum solids removed, depending on their tank size and the daily load discharged into them. Some tanks need to be pumped out every 2 years, but others may need it only once every 10 years. (Homeowners who claim they never have pumped out their septic tanks probably have an incomplete system that doesn't have a leaching field and discharges directly into ditches, streams, lakes, or agricultural drain tile lines.) Tanks should be inspected annually to see if pumping is necessary. A probe with a 3-inch square-shaped foot can be used to check the level of the scum layer. If the bottom of the layer is within 3 inches of the bottom of the outlet tee, or baffle, the tank should be pumped out. A pole with an old bath towel wrapped around the bottom 3 feet can be used to measure the sludge depth. Pump out tank if sludge is within 12 inches of outlet tee, or baffle. *Note: Chemical additives are not needed for proper septic tank operation and, in some cases, can harm the tank.*

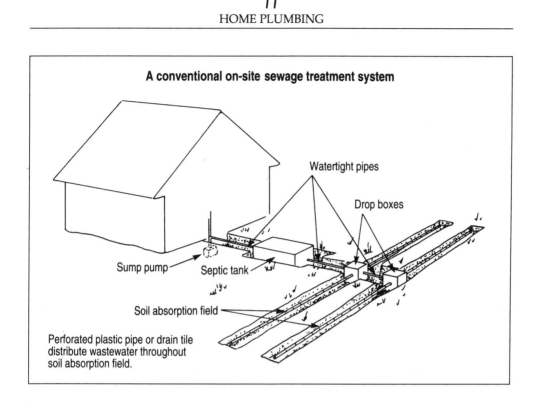

A conventional on-site sewage treatment system

Watertight pipes

Drop boxes

Sump pump

Septic tank

Soil absorption field

Perforated plastic pipe or drain tile distribute wastewater throughout soil absorption field.

Special advice: After pumping out, the condition of the tank's inlet and outlet tees, or baffles, should be inspected and replaced if damaged. *Never enter, or allow anyone else to enter, a septic tank unless a continuous supply of fresh air is pumped into the tank and a strong rope is attached to the person entering the tank.* Adequate help should be available at all times in case it becomes necessary to lift a person out of the tank. Maintenance of the leaching field is limited to checking the distribution box or drop boxes twice a year. (Drop boxes provide a simple method of distributing flow on sloping sites. If used, inlets to the most heavily loaded trenches can be blocked off for 6 to 12 months to overcome effects of unbalanced loading.) There is no need to wash or disinfect a tank after pumping. It is also not necessary to leave some sludge in the tank, or add special chemicals, to get the tank started after pumping.

Helpful hint: Septic tanks are designed to trap and store solid materials, not carry them away. To avoid sludge buildup or clogged sewer lines leading to the tank or the tank's inlet and outlet parts, do not flush items such as cat litter, rags, sticks, plastic disposable diaper linings, high-strength paper products, and other nondecomposable products into the system.

HOME HEATING AND COOLING

●●●●●●●●●●●●●

51 Thermostat Doesn't Work

Problem: Thermostat for home heat and cooling system does not work, or does not work properly.

Background: A properly functioning thermostat is the brain that regulates heating and cooling to maintain comfortable temperatures in a home. The complexity of your thermostat depends on whether your home has a furnace only, or a furnace and central air conditioner, and whether it is a programmable set-back model. Set-back thermostats automatically adjust the system at certain periods to save energy, either by dropping temperature during the heating season, or increasing it during the cooling season. Thermostats are quite reliable, but may not work because they are mis-installed, fall out of adjustment, need cleaning, or because components malfunction.

What to do: You can use the simple tests outlined below to determine whether your thermostat is defective. See entry 52 for malfunctions caused by dust or poor contacts; see entry 53 for adjustment-related problems.

If the problem is that the system fails to produce heat, turn off the power to the furnace, then remove the thermostat from wall. Disconnect 1 wire from the back of the thermostat. Turn on the power to the furnace. Touch the loose wire to the wire still connected. If the burner comes on, the thermostat is defective and needs to be replaced.

If the system is not cooling, turn off the power to the cooling system. Remove the thermostat from wall. Disconnect the wire from the Y terminal. Turn on the power to the cooling system. Touch the loose wire to the R terminal. If the compressor starts, the thermostat is defective and should be replaced. (Some systems have a time delay, so allow at least 2 minutes.)

Special advice: If you suspect something is wrong with your thermostat, make sure the problem is not with the furnace or air-conditioning equipment (see entries 54 and 59). Make sure the equipment is receiving power by checking for a blown fuse or tripped circuit breaker at both the main service panel and any secondary circuit boxes. Also check the furnace power switch and the air-conditioner condenser switch (located outdoors on the unit) to see that they are on. If the equipment has been working, check your owner's manual for any special start-up procedures—especially if an electronic-ignition furnace has "locked out" (or become temporarily disabled), or if the pilot has gone out on equipment with pilot lights.

Helpful hint: Before testing the thermostat, make sure the connections inside of the unit are making contact. With the power to the furnace turned off, tighten all mounting and terminal screws and repair any broken wires.

• • •

52 Thermostat Malfunctions

Problem: Thermostat is not working properly because of dirt or corrosion.

Background: A common problem causing poor thermostat operation is dust and dirt accumulation on the

unit's sensing element or contact points. A layer of dust can affect the speed with which the thermostat senses a change in temperature. This may allow the home to become too cold before the thermostat instructs the heating system to come on, or it may allow the home to become too warm before turning off the system.

What to do: Older thermostats, particularly those operating forced-air systems that move large volumes of air, should be cleaned regularly. To clean, remove the cover and use a soft brush to dust the components or use a vacuum near the unit, being careful not to damage sensitive parts. If the dirt is caked on, you may need to call a service technician. Some older thermostats may operate with contact points instead of a mercury-filled glass bulb. The two metal strips are installed parallel to each other, and make or break the electrical circuit to the heating unit. With

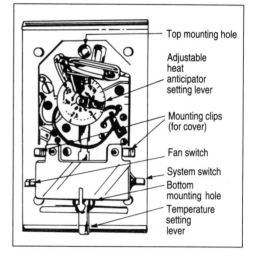

Top mounting hole

Adjustable heat anticipator setting lever

Mounting clips (for cover)

Fan switch

System switch

Bottom mounting hole

Temperature setting lever

power off, gently blow out the dust or wipe these strips with a soft cloth.

Special advice: If the contact points are corroded, they can be cleaned by pulling a piece of crocus cloth or bond paper (such as a business card) through the points. If this doesn't do the trick, consider replacing it with a new unit or calling a service technician.

Helpful hint: Whenever thermostat wires must be disconnected from the unit, make sure they do not fall back into the opening in the wall. A good way to make sure this doesn't happen is to wrap the end of the wire around the center of a pencil.

● ● ●

53 Thermostat Needs Adjustment

Problem: Thermostat works, but turns furnace on and off rapidly, causes major swings in temperature, or shows readings other than the setting.

Background: Normally, properly installed thermostats require little or no attention. However, some common problems can often be remedied by the homeowner, thereby saving the expense of a service call. If the thermostat has been recently installed, consult the instructions that came with the unit. For other thermostat problems, see entries 51 and 52.

What to do: If the thermostat turns the furnace on and off relatively often, the problem is likely that the burner-on period is too short. Inside the thermostat is a heat anticipator lever which can be set to a range of scale markings. Adjust the lever one scale mark higher. Wait at least several hours for the thermostat to stabilize. If the thermostat allows major swings in temperature, the problem likely is a "burner-on" period that is too long. In this case, adjust the heat anticipator lever one scale mark lower. Again, wait several hours for the system to stabilize.

Special advice: If the thermostat setting and the thermometer reading disagree, the thermostat may not be level, it may be affected by drafts or radiant heat, or it may be out of calibration. To check whether it is level, place a bubble level or a plumb line against the unit. If the thermostat is being affected by drafts and heat, it may need to be relocated. If it is out of calibration, read the unit's instructions to find out how to adjust it, or call a technician.

Helpful hint: Normally a thermostat should be placed at least 5 feet off of the floor, away from sources of heat (including sunlight), and on an interior wall. It should also be positioned away from corners and dead spots behind doors and in closets. It should not be located on walls that have ducts or pipes inside them, and should be protected from air flow within the wall. Plug any holes cut into the attic or crawl space for plumbing and wiring, and plug the hole behind the thermostat where the low voltage wires emerge.

• • •

54 Furnace Doesn't Work

Problem: Furnace is dead, or doesn't turn on when the thermostat is raised.

Background: What are often thought to be furnace emergencies are caused by the thermostat being set or operated wrong, by having the power to the furnace cut off, or by not having fuel or a working pilot light. (*Important: If you detect gas odor in your home or in the furnace area, take immediate precautions; see entry 5.*) For thermostat-related problems, check entries 51, 52, and 53.

What to do: First double-check to be sure that power is reaching the furnace. Check the circuit breakers or fuses at the main service box. If reset breakers or replaced fuses blow again, call a service technician. Also check to see that any switches on or near the furnace are turned on. Be sure that the thermostat is set in the "heat" position, and that it is set above room temperature. If the furnace doesn't come on after an inter-

val, check the furnace itself. If you have a gas furnace, the gas valve should be turned to "on." If you have an oil furnace, check the fuel level in the tank. If the furnace has a pilot light, check to make sure that it is lit. If not, relight it carefully, following the instructions in the owner's manual or on the unit.

(*Warning: If you smell gas, leave the area immediately and call a technician.* The lighting instructions for a gas furnace should explain the procedure to use to determine whether the gas valve is good. If the test procedure indicates the gas valve is bad, turn off furnace gas valve and main gas valve and call a technician. Also call for help if the pilot light does not stay lit after several tries.)

Special advice: Most furnace controls will have a reset switch. If the furnace starts after the reset switch is pushed, but shuts off again, call a technician. Gas furnaces equipped with an electronic ignition device, instead of a pilot light, have a gas valve designed for slow opening. It first opens part way to let just enough gas through for safe ignition of the burners. After a few seconds it opens fully to allow proper flame height. The burners should light within 2 seconds after the gas valve opens. If air in the valve and lines prevents the flame from being established within 6 seconds or so, the system will go into "lock-out." To reset, wait 1 minute and turn the thermostat to a setting below room temperature. Then turn back up to a setting above room temperature;

this should re-start the ignition cycle.

Helpful hint: If the furnace works, but heat is not circulating, the problem may be with the blower or the blower belt (see entry 55). If the flame on burner is yellow or blue, or lifts off of the burner, call for a technician to adjust. Check your owner's manual for annual maintenance suggestions and keep the furnace and its components free of lint or dirt accumulation.

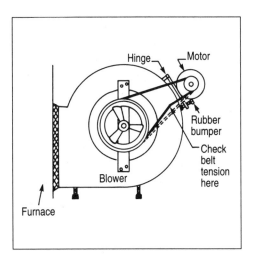

● ● ●

55 Furnace Makes Noises

Problem: Furnace makes unfamiliar noises when operating.

Background: Sometimes homeowners think their forced-air furnaces need to be replaced because they make strange noises. But the cause may be a simple mechanical problem with the motor or fan within the blower system. Sometimes making simple adjustments and/or replacing a part will solve a strange noise problem.

What to do: Turn off the power to the furnace, remove access panels, and make a careful examination of the blower area. Check to make sure that the drive belt between the motor and the blower has proper tension, is in alignment, and is not cracked.

Also check the pulley on the motor, making sure that it is not loose on the shaft, has worn grooves, or is dirty. If loose, retighten any set-screws. If worn or dirty, remove the belt, clean the pulley, and sand down its interior sides. Also check the pulley on the blower fan. Spin the blower to check for sound which may be caused by something inside. If the fan is rubbing against the housing, it needs to be adjusted and your best bet is to call a technician. Push and pull on blower pulley to check for end-play. If excessive, shaft collars need to be adjusted.

Special advice: A blower that needs oil may also make noises. Follow owner manual instructions to oil. Sometimes oil-less bearings wear out and need replacement. To see if the motor is making the noise, remove the belt and run the motor; the motor may simply need oiling, but motor bearings may still make noise. If so, decide if you can live with the noise or if you want to replace the motor. A dirty furnace filter can also cause noise; clean the filter as recommended.

Helpful hint: If the burner of a gas furnace makes an unusual noise, the gas input amount may not be correct, or it may be getting too much primary air. In either case, contact a service technician. Also, contact a technician immediately if the walls or windows in your home sweat excessively. The furnace may not be getting enough ventilation or the flue pipe may be blocked (see entry 7).

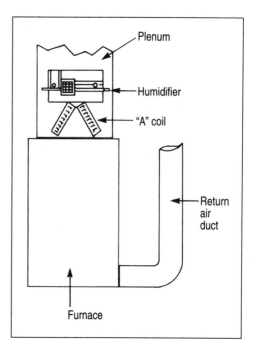

• • •

56 Central Humidifier Overflows

Problem: The humidifier installed in a forced-air furnace is leaking or overflowing.

Background: A furnace-installed humidifier can overflow because it has a defective float valve, a defective float valve seat, because the unit is not mounted level or in the right position in the furnace, or for other reasons. Sometimes a humidifier may create minor overflow when the media pad needs replacement or is rubbing against the side of the unit.

What to do: First check to see that the humidifier unit is level both horizontally and vertically, using a carpenter's level. If the unit is not level, adjust the mounting. Check the float valve and its adjustment to be sure that it is set for the right water level. (Also check to see that the float itself is not defective; if it is leaking water it must be replaced.) Inside the float valve mechanism there may be a small black rubber button that seals the valve water outlet. If the button shows wear from water erosion, reverse the button or replace it. Then make sure the button seats properly and evenly on the float-valve water outlet.

Special advice: In some cases a central humidifier may be installed incorrectly so that its opening is located inside the "A" frame of the air-conditioner coil in the plenum of the furnace. In this case, overflowing may be the result of the high static air pressure in this location and the unit should be relocated above the "A" coil.

Helpful hint: When replacing the media pad on the media wheel of the humidifier, make sure that it does not extend past the wheel edges. Do not turn the wheel while it is attached to the motor; damage to the gears may result. Use a solution of 1 part household vinegar and 3 parts water, or a commercial mineral dissolving cleaner to dissolve lime buildup in the humidifier.

• • •

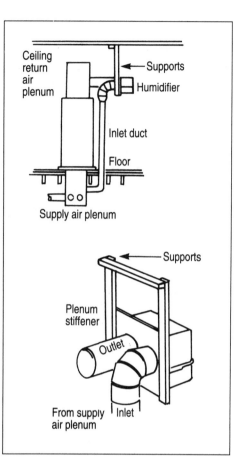

57 | Central Humidifier Is Noisy

Problem: When furnace is on, central humidifier makes an unfamiliar noise.

Background: Some noise will naturally be produced by anything that moves air. However, if the central humidifier on your forced-air furnace makes an unusual sound, there may be specific causes that can be corrected. Turn off the electricity at the fuse box or breaker panel or unplug the unit. Then close the saddle valve, which feeds water to the humidifier, and remove any drain tubing so the unit can be taken apart and inspected.

What to do: Remove the lower unit by unfastening latches and pour out any remaining water. If the humidifier was installed using a plenum stiffener, check it to make sure it is securely fastened to the plenum and that all the screws are tight. Then make sure the humidifier is securely attached to the plenum stiffener. Next check to be sure that any setscrew in the hub of the media wheel motor shaft is tight. If not, tighten it. Also check to see that the media

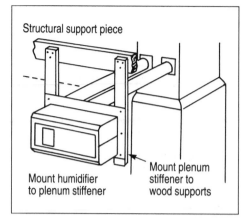

Structural support piece

Mount humidifier to plenum stiffener

Mount plenum stiffener to wood supports

58 Room Air Conditioner Quits

Problem: Air conditioner does not operate, or turns off and on sporadically.

Background: Regular care and light maintenance of compact room air conditioners helps assure longer service life and lower operating costs. Most important for maximum cooling is the regular cleaning of the permanent, washable filter, which removes dust, lint, and other airborne particles. It should be checked at least every 30 days of operation. The unit should also be inspected annually by yourself or a technician.

What to do: If the air conditioner is not operating, first check to see if its cord is properly plugged into the outlet. Check the main electrical panel to see if a fuse has blown, or if a breaker has tripped. If this is not the problem, turn on a light to find out if the local power supply has failed. If it has not, check to see if the air conditioner has been accidently turned off.

If the air conditioner operates intermittently (turns off and on) or does not cool the room, check to see if anything is blocking the front of the unit. Close the doors to adjoining rooms and if the thermostat is set at less than the coldest position, turn it to that position. Also check the filter and coils for dirt accumulation. Be

wheel is still round. If it isn't, it must be reshaped or replaced. Check the alignment of the wheel, and also make sure there are no bent blades in the blower or the motor fan.

Special advice: If the noise persists, it may be due to the rough edges that were created when the ductwork was cut to mount the humidifier. If these edges are rough, straighten them. Also check the water pressure to the humidifier. If it's too high, it may cause a vibration noise in the water line (between the humidifier and the saddle valve). This can be remedied by cutting down the flow of water at the saddle valve, or by fastening the water line to a ceiling joist or wall.

Helpful hint: To find out if the noise is coming from the motor, remove the media wheel, reassemble and turn on unit. If the motor is causing the noise, install a replacement or call a technician to do the job.

● ● ●

aware that if the air conditioner is being fed power through a long extension cord, it may not be getting enough power to operate properly.

Special advice: You should be able to remove the permanent, washable-type filter, and clean it by using a vacuum cleaner. If the filter is extremely dirty or clogged, clean it in warm water with a normal amount of detergent and dry it before replacing. Plastic parts of the unit may also be cleaned with a soapy water solution, using a soft cloth.

Helpful hint: Every year the coils and condensate water passages should be inspected and cleaned, if necessary. Although the compressor is the hermetically sealed type and the fan motor is likely to be permanently oiled, these parts should also be checked annually to ensure that they are in good operating condition.

● ● ●

59 Central Air Conditioner Quits

Problem: Central air conditioning doesn't come on, doesn't cool, or makes noises.

Background: An air-conditioning system pumps heat out of your home. There are two types of central air conditioners: the package system

and the split system. The package system has the compressor, outdoor coil, indoor coil, fan, and blower motors in the same housing outside the home; it's connected to the ducts in the home through an outside wall. The split system has the compressor, fan motor, and coil outdoors. The coil and blower motor (usually an existing furnace blower is used) is indoors and refrigerant lines run between the two sections. Your air conditioner, unless it is used in conjunction with a gas or oil furnace, may also be equipped to provide auxiliary heating with what is called a strip heating system. This system warms the air by blowing it across an electric resistance heating element.

What to do: Many times air conditioners do not start up or work properly because the electrical power is not turned on. Check the circuit breakers or fuses and load-center handles in both indoor and outdoor locations. Study the user's guide. Make sure that the setting on the thermostat is set to "cool" or "auto" and that the fan switch is set on "auto" or "on" for continuous operation. The setting should be below room temperature. Check the coil outside to be sure that the fan is running. Make sure grilles, registers, and indoor filters are not restricting air flow. (Dirty filters are the most common cause of inadequate cooling and compressor failures.)

Call a technician if you hear new, unusual noises or if the air conditioner is short-cycling (turning on and off rapidly) and not cooling properly. When performing any maintenance, be sure to shut off the electrical power. But otherwise manufacturers suggest you leave the power to the outdoor unit on at all times. To prevent damage to the compressor, do not use the air conditioner until electrical power has been turned on for at least 6 hours.

Special advice: Never use the outdoor coil as a stand for garden hoses or tools. To assure free air flow, keep the outdoor coil clean and free of grass clippings, weeds, and other debris. Keep fences and shrubs at least 2 feet away from it. Clean and wax the cabinet with car polish to protect the finish. Manufacturers recommend not covering an outdoor unit with any all-weather cover unless it is a ventilated type or is made of breathable fabric that will allow moisture to evaporate rapidly. A cover that holds moisture may cause more rust and other damage than normal exposure to weather.

Helpful hint: Replace glass fiber throw-away filters when dirty. Clean plastic fiber or foam filters by soaking them in a mild detergent and rinsing them with cold water. Aluminum mesh filters can be washed with detergent and water, but they should be recoated according to the manufacturer's instructions; they won't filter dust or dirt as effectively without the adhesive coating.

• • •

60 Radiator Valve Leaks

Problem: Radiator valve leaks around stem, dripping onto floor.

Background: If you have an old-style radiator that has a valve which is leaking, take care of the problem as soon as possible. The leak can damage the floor, and even the ceiling below the radiator. Often valves

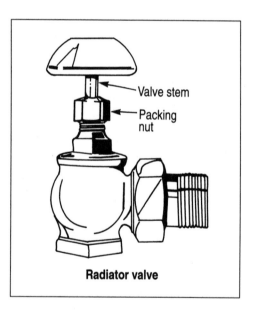

Radiator valve

leak around the stem because the packing inside the packing nut is worn or insufficient, or because the packing nut itself is loose. First try tightening the packing nut. If the leak persists, you will probably have to repack the valve stem. Many older radiator valves were built so that the packing nut can be raised without lowering the pressure in the radiator. In a hot-water system, where the valve permits water or steam to escape after the valve is closed and the packing nut is loosened, the level of water must be lowered below the height of the valve by opening the system's drain cock. With a steam system, first reduce the pressure by allowing the boiler to cool.

What to do: Two forms of packing material can be used to repack the valve stem: different size washers or packing cord. If you use washers, loosen the screw holding the valve handle, remove the handle and withdraw the packing nut from the stem. Take out the old packing and slip the new packing washers over the stem. (Use the right number and size of washers to fill the packing space in the nut.) If using cord, wrap enough around the valve stem to fill the packing space in the nut. The nut should be tight enough to keep water and steam from escaping, but not so tight that it keeps excessive friction on the stem when the valve is turned.

Special advice: With a steam-heating system, let the fire go out, or at least have a low head of steam, before starting to work on the valves. After the system is cool enough to work on, close the valve tightly and unscrew the packing nut at the base of the stem. Pack the space between the inside of the nut and stem with metallic packing compound, using a small screwdriver. It may be easier to pack the nut if it is removed from the stem. To do this, remove the handle and lift the nut from the stem. After the nut has been repacked, screw it down tightly and refill the system, following the instructions in the owner's manual.

Helpful hint: If you are unsure about proper procedures with an older heating system, call a heating equipment specialist. Don't tamper unnecessarily with controls or mechanisms and have a qualified technician perform major repairs, replacements, and seasonal maintenance.

HOME APPLIANCES

●●●●●●●●●●●●●

61 | Water Heater Leaks

Problem: Frying or sizzling noises are heard when the heater's burner comes on.

Background: The water heater tank may be leaking onto the burner, or condensation water may be dropping into the burner area. Whenever the heater is filled with cold water, a certain amount of condensation will form while the burner is on. This usually happens 1) when a new heater is filled with cold water for the first time, 2) when gas burns and water vapor is produced in heaters, particularly in high-efficiency models where flue temperatures are lower, and 3) when large amounts of hot water are used in a short time and the refill water is very cold.

What to do: Heaters with tank leaks should be replaced. However, don't assume a water heater is leaking until there has been enough time for the water in the tank to warm up. A

water heater may appear to be leaking when, in fact, the water is condensation. Excessive condensation can cause water to run down the flue tube onto the main burner of a gas-fired heater and put out the pilot. This condition may be noticed during the winter and early spring

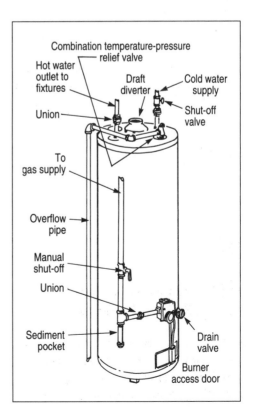

Combination temperature-pressure relief valve
Hot water outlet to fixtures
Draft diverter
Cold water supply
Union
Shut-off valve
To gas supply
Overflow pipe
Manual shut-off
Union
Sediment pocket
Drain valve
Burner access door

months when incoming water temperatures are lowest. After the water in the tank has warmed up (about 1 to 2 hours), the problem should disappear.

Special advice: If condensation is heavy, also check the venting system of a gas-fired heater. Good venting is essential for the heater to operate properly, as well as to carry away the combustion and water-vapor products. Inspect the venting system once a year, looking for obstructions blocking combustion and ventilation air flow, or damage or deterioration which could cause improper venting or leakage of combustion products. If discovered, have the flue and venting cleaned or replaced before resuming operation of the heater. See entry 7.

Helpful hint: An undersized water heater will cause more condensation to form. The heater must be sized properly to meet home demands, including dishwashers, washing machines, and showers.

• • •

62 Water Heater Makes Noises

Problem: Water heater makes unusual noises, which may include sizzling, popping, crackling, pounding, and rumbling sounds.

Background: Certain noises from a water heater may be normal, such as the expansion and contraction of metal parts during heating-up and cooling-down periods. Sizzling and popping sounds may be caused within the burner area by the formation of normal condensation during heating and cooling periods. Sediment buildup on the bottom of the tank may also create various noises (and if left in the tank, may cause premature tank failure).

What to do: If water heater is making crackling, sizzling, or popping noises, check to determine whether it is a leak or normal condensation (see entry 61). In some cases the temperature-pressure (TP) relief valve may be dripping because the water supply system has pressure-reducing valves, check valves or back-

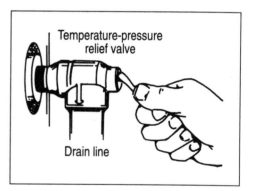

Temperature-pressure relief valve

Drain line

flow preventers. When these devices are not equipped with an internal bypass and no other measures are taken, they can cause the water system to close so it does not allow for the expansion of heated water. In this case the TP valve will drip to relieve the excess pressure. Call a technician to install a bypass and/or an expansion tank to relieve the pressure from thermal expansion.

In some cases, a TP valve may leak because the water heater temperature is set too high; in other cases, it is because the TP valve is bad. Too high of a temperature setting can also cause pounding and rumbling or a surging sound in the heater.

Special advice: Sediment buildup in the tank can cause water heater noises as water droplets get under the sediment and convert to steam when heated. Drain the tank to clean; if the problem remains, contract a technician to do a professional cleaning. Similar sounds can come from electric water heaters and are caused by scale-encrusted heating elements; in this case, the elements can be replaced. Sediment buildup can be reduced by regularly draining a few quarts of water every month from the drain valve at the lower front of the tank.

Helpful hint: The TP relief valve should be manually operated at least once a year. Check your owner's manual for the recommended procedure. Make sure no one is near the outlet of the discharge line, and that extremely hot water discharged will not cause damage when discharged. (If the valve continues to release water after manually operating it, close the cold water inlet to the heater, following draining instructions in your manual, and contact a technician to replace the TP valve.)

● ● ●

63 Water Heater Overheats

Problem: Water heater doesn't shut off, causing overheating.

Background: An overheating water heater may cause boiling noises to come from inside the tank, steam to pop from hot water faucets, or hot water to back up into the cold water supply. (See entry 62 for causes of other water heater noises.) Normally the temperature-pressure (TP) relief valve protects the heater from excessive temperatures and pressures. However, it may have been improperly installed or become defective.

What to do: If a runaway water heater is suspected, turn off the burner and use a thermometer to check the water at a hot-water faucet. (Some heaters may be equipped with an automatic gas shutoff system actuated by high water temperature.) If the reading is above what the setting on the heater should produce, the heater's thermostat may be defective. Reset it if necessary; if that doesn't help, call a technician. After the tank has been allowed to cool, check to see that the TP valve is working.

Special advice: Hot water presents a scalding hazard that varies according to the amount of time exposed and age of the persons involved. (Scalding may occur at different temperatures for children, elderly, infirm, or physically handicapped.) The Consumer Product Safety Commission recommends water temperatures be kept at 130° or lower.

Helpful hint: If persons potentially subject to scalding hazards are present in your home, or if local codes require a certain water temperature, lower the temperature setting as low as possible to meet your needs. Also consider installing some type of tempering device, such as a mixing valve, at hot water taps used by at-risk people, or at the water heater.

● ● ●

64 Water from Heater Smells

Problem: Hot water from water heater has odor.

Background: At least one anode rod is installed in every water heater to provide corrosion protection for the tank. Certain water conditions will cause a reaction between this rod and the water, causing the hot water to assume a "rotten egg" smell. The odor results from hydrogen sulfide gas becoming dissolved in the water.

What to do: For the odor to develop, four factors must be present (1) a concentration of sulfate in the supply water, (2) little or no dissolved oxygen in the water, (3) a sulfate-reducing bacteria within the water heater (a harmless bacteria nontoxic to humans), and (4) an excess of active hydrogen in the tank. *To remedy, do not simply remove the anode(s), leaving the tank unprotected.* The odor may be reduced or eliminated in some water heaters by replacing the anode(s) with types that have less active material, and then chlorinating the water heater tank and all hot water lines. Check with the manufacturer or dealer for replacement anodes and chlorination equipment.

Special advice: Hydrogen is generated by the corrosion-protective anode, and hydrogen gas can build up in a hot water system unused for 2 weeks or more. This gas is extremely flammable and explosive. As a precautionary measure, open the hot water faucet for several minutes at the kitchen sink before connecting any electrical appliance to the hot water system (such as a dishwasher or a washing machine). If hydrogen gas is present, there will likely be a sound similar to air escaping through the pipe. *Do not smoke or have any open flame near the faucet when you open it.*

Helpful hint: If smelly water persists after anode replacement and chlorination treatment, consider installing continuous chlorination and filtering conditioning equipment to reduce the problem.

● ● ●

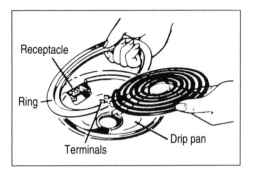

65 Stove Elements Defective

Problem: Plug-in surface element doesn't work and needs replacement.

Background: Plug-in heating element units can often be removed for cleaning and for replacement. (Some newer tilt-lock surface units are not designed to be removed from the top; however, they can be lifted upward about 6 inches and they will lock in an upward facing position.) Replacing 3-wire elements on older

ranges is more complicated; consult your owner's manual, appliance repair books, or appliance part retailer for advice. Before replacing an element, make sure it is plugged in solidly, controls are properly set, and that trim rings and drip pans are securely set into the range top.

What to do: Be sure all controls are turned off and surface units are cool before attempting to lift or remove them. Lift the plug-in unit about 1 inch above the trim ring, enough to grasp it and pull it out. Don't lift the

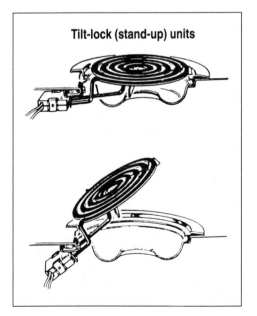

Tilt-lock (stand-up) units

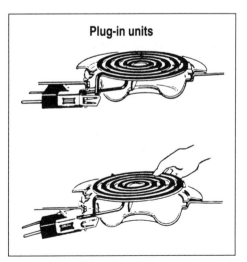

Plug-in units

plug-in unit more than 1 inch. If you do, it may not lie flat on the trim ring when you plug it back in. (Repeated lifting of the plug-in unit more than 1 inch above the trim ring can permanently damage the receptacle.) To confirm that the element is defective before you buy a new one, try another element of the same size that you know is working. If it also works when plugged into the receptacle where the nonworking element was, you will know the element in question is defective.

Special advice: To replace a plug-in element unit, first place the drip pan, then the trim ring into the surface unit cavity so the unit receptacle can be seen through the opening in the pan. Insert the terminals of the plug-in unit through the opening in the drip pan and into the receptacle. Guide the element into place so it fits evenly into the trim ring, making sure the drip pan is under the trim ring.

Helpful hint: Don't attempt to clean plug-in surface units in a dishwasher or immerse them in liquids of any kind. Also, don't bend the plug-in unit plug terminals or attempt to clean, adjust, or in any way repair the plug-in receptacle.

● ● ●

66 Oven Thermostat Faulty

Problem: Oven thermostat setting is off and needs adjustment.

Background: If, when using the time given in recipes, foods consistently brown too little or too much, the oven thermostat may be out of adjustment. Over time oven thermostats may drift from the factory setting; 5- to 10-minute differences in timing between an old and a new oven are not uncommon. To correct the situation, on many ovens you can make a simple adjustment in the thermostat (oven temperature) knob. Small adjustments can be made a little at a time, or a precise temperature tester (available at an appliance parts store) can be used to determine temperature inside the oven so you can adjust the thermostat knob accordingly.

What to do: Pull the oven temperature knob off of its shaft and look at the back of the knob and note the setting of the pointer before making any adjustment. To increase the temperature, move the pointer toward "high" or "raise"; to decrease, turn toward "low" or "lower." Each notch should change the temperature 10°. On some knobs you have to hold the skirt of the knob firmly in one hand and turn the knob with the other hand to move the pointer. The pointer is designed to be difficult to move but you can loosen it by slightly lifting up the end of the pointer with a thin screwdriver, knife blade, or similar instrument. On other knobs you may have to loosen 2 screws on the back to move the pointer 1 notch in the desired direction. Replace the knob to the shaft, and recheck the oven's performance before making additional adjustments.

Special advice: If you are using a temperature tester to calibrate the oven, allow the oven element to cycle on at least twice. Then, with the oven set at a specific temperature, take 4 readings to get an average temperature. Take 2 readings when the element cycles on, and 2 readings when it cycles off. Add up the readings and divide the sum by 4 to get the average temperature. The average should be within 25° of the knob setting. If it isn't, recalibrate the setting.

Helpful hint: When testing the oven temperature, do not rely on the inexpensive thermometers you can buy at discount stores. Their readings will not provide the accuracy needed.

• • •

Oven Light Burns Out

Problem: Range oven light does not work when switched on.

Background: If the oven light will not work, first make sure the stove is getting power. Check to see that the plug from the range is completely inserted in the electrical outlet. Also the circuit breaker in your house may have been tripped, or a fuse may have been blown. The light bulb may also be loose in its socket.

What to do: Before replacing the oven lamp bulb, disconnect the electric power for your range at the main fuse or circuit breaker panel. Let the lamp cover and bulb cool completely before attempting to remove or replace them. On many stove models, the oven lamp bulb is covered with a removable glass cover which is held in place with a bail-shaped wire. (On other models, you may have to remove screws to take off the glass cover.) With the bail-type, hold your hand under the glass cover so it doesn't fall when released. With your fingers (on the same hand), firmly push back the wire bail until it clears the cover. Lift off the cover and try tightening the bulb, in case it was loose. If this doesn't work, replace the bulb with a home appliance bulb of the same wattage.

Special advice: To replace the glass cover, place it into the groove of the lamp receptacle. Pull the wire bail forward to the center of the cover until it snaps into place. When in place, the wire should hold the cover firmly. Be sure the wire bail is in the depression in the center of the cover.

After the cover is in place, restore electric power to the range.

Helpful hint: If a new bulb doesn't work, the problem may be that the switch operating the oven light is defective. Call for a technician or consult an appliance parts retailer.

• • •

68 Clothes Washer Quits

Problem: Clothes washer is not working, or does not work properly.

Background: Clothes washers use 3 basic systems, all controlled by elec-tricity: water fill, water drain, and drive. Before calling for service, check for the following possible problems. If the washer still doesn't work right, check detailed appliance-repair handbooks available, or call a technician. If the machine won't fill, for example, the problem may be dirty water-sediment screens, defective water-mixing valve solenoids, or a defective water temperature switch. If the water won't shut off, the problem could be dirt inside the mixing valve, a bad water-level control switch, defective timer, or a short circuit. If the machine won't agitate or spin, a faulty water-level control switch or agitator solenoid may be the problem. No-spin prob-lems also may be caused by a faulty drive unit or timer. If the machine doesn't drain, the problem may be "suds lock," a water pump belt, or a damaged water pump impeller.

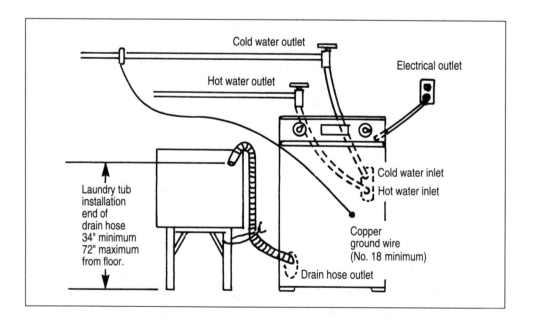

What to do: If the clothes washer won't fill or agitate and won't spin or drain, or stops, make sure that the power cord is plugged into an electrical outlet, that a fuse hasn't blown or a circuit breaker tripped, and that the control knob is not turned "off." If the washer fills slowly, make sure that the inlet hoses are not plugged or kinked, that the water faucets are fully on, and that water pressure is sufficient. If the unit won't fill or agitate, also double-check to be sure that the inlet hoses are not plugged or kinked, and that the water faucets are turned on. If the washer won't spin or drain, also check that the lid is not open and the water faucets are turned on. If the unit drains when it is not running, make sure that the drain hose is not lower than the washer or is not fitted too tightly in any standpipe being used.

Special advice: If your clothes washer shakes and vibrates when in use, check the following. Make sure that the front legs are not loose, that shipping straps are completely removed, that the washer is level, that the load is balanced, and that the floor is strong enough. The floor beneath the washer should be level, with no more than 2 inches slope under the entire washer. The floor must be strong enough to support the weight of the filled washer, about 315 pounds.

Helpful hint: A clothes washer should drain into a 20-gallon tub or a 2-inch diameter standpipe. If the washer is connected to a floor drain, a siphon break must be installed. The drain should be able to carry away 17 gallons of water per minute. The end of the drain hose should be more than 34 inches, but less than 72 inches, above the base of the washer. If you use less than a 2-inch diameter standpipe, there must be an air gap around the hose inside the standpipe to a siphoning action from occurring.

● ● ●

69 Dishwasher Malfunctions

Problem: Dishwasher won't work, or doesn't operate properly.

Background: To do a good job dishwashers need water that is hot enough, supplied with enough pressure, and that is not too hard. Manufacturers recommend water temperature be at least 140°, though some energy specialists say 130° is hot enough. Because a dishwasher fills with wash or rinse water for a limited length of time, it will not get enough water if the water pressure is too low. Pressure should be between 20 and 120 pounds per square inch. A simple test for pressure is to close all other faucets and put a half-gallon container under a fully opened hot water faucet nearest the dishwasher. It should be full in less than 14 seconds. Review the following suggestions before calling a technician.

What to do: If the dishwasher will not run, make sure it is receiving electrical power and that the controls are in the "on" position. If the unit doesn't fill, check first to see that the water is not shut off; the valve on the incoming water line should be in the open position. Also check to see that the unit's float is not stuck. (To prevent the float inside the unit from sticking in the up position where it stops the water from filling, periodically lift it out and clean around the tube it fits into. Make sure the float moves up and down freely after it is replaced in the tube.) A small amount of clean water in the bottom of the unit after each cycle is normal and serves to lubricate the water seal. However, excess water in the bottom may be caused by an improperly installed drain hose. If water won't drain from the machine, check to see if the house drain is plugged or if the drain air gap (if used) is stopped up and needs cleaning. If the dishwasher leaks, it may be because it does not sit level or because a detergent used has caused excessive sudsing.

Special advice: If the dishwasher produces excessive noise, make sure dishes are loaded properly (see your owner's manual) and that the unit is sitting level. Noise can also be caused by hard objects—such as fruit pits, measuring spoons, or bottle caps—that have fallen into the pump openings in the bottom of the unit. To clean, make sure machine is cool, then remove the bolt above the spray arm. Remove any objects that are in or around the pump openings, and replace the spray arm and bolt. (Note: It is important not to let small metallic items, such as pot-handle screws, fall into the pump openings since they may cause serious damage to the pump parts.)

Helpful hint: Plugged spray arms, or spray arms that do not turn freely, can keep dishes from getting clean. If necessary, clean out any food fragments that may have collected in the openings. Also check it to see that they rotate freely after loading to make sure some utensil is not preventing them from turning.

•••

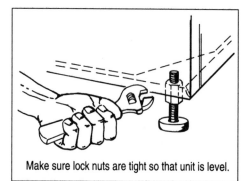

Make sure lock nuts are tight so that unit is level.

70 Refrigerator Malfunctions

Problem: Refrigerator doesn't work, or doesn't work properly.

Background: Newer refrigerators are largely self-sufficient, and many models have electronic monitor and diagnostic systems. Added features, such as ice makers, complicate the mechanical system and require more attention. Keep your owner's manual handy; if you don't have one, order a copy to have on hand. For efficient operation, try to avoid locating the unit next to a range, a heating vent, or where the sun shines directly on it. The tips below include some suggestions for handling minor problems you can correct yourself. For other tips, see your owner's manual, or contact a qualified technician.

What to do: If there is no touch-panel response, or if the unit does not operate, check to see if the interior light is on. If not, the unit may not be plugged in at the wall outlet. If the plug is secure and the refrigerator still doesn't operate, plug a lamp or small appliance into the same outlet to see if there is a tripped circuit breaker or burned-out fuse. Also check to be sure that the temperature control is not in the "off" position. (Note that the unit may be in a defrost cycle, in which the motor doesn't operate for about a half hour.) If the unit is getting power, and an interior light doesn't come on, a light bulb may be burned out or the door switch may be defective. If the motor runs for long periods, it may be caused by large amounts of food placed into the unit to be cooled or frozen, by hot weather, frequent door openings,

because a door has been left open, or because the temperature control is set too low. The grille and coils may also need cleaning; clean at least once a year to remove dust from the fin-and-tube assembly either on the back or underneath the unit. A special brush designed for the job is available at appliance parts stores.

If the refrigerator vibrates or rattles, it is probably not resting solidly on the floor. If the floor is weak or uneven, the roller screws or front leveling legs may need adjusting. If the door doesn't close properly, check to see that the door gasket on the hinge side isn't sticking or folding over. To fix, put a small amount of petroleum jelly on the face of the gasket. If water leaks onto floor under the unit, the drain from the freezer may be clogged. On newer models, remove ice from the freezer bottom and clean the drain by flushing a solution of 1 teaspoon baking soda and 2 cups hot water through the drain line using a meat baster. If your automatic icemaker doesn't work, make sure its feeler arm is not in the "off" position or pointing upward. Also be sure that the water supply is connected, turned on and not clogged, and that ice cubes haven't piled up on the bin causing it to shut off. If cubes don't dispense, irregular ice clumps in the bin may be the cause.

Special advice: Generally, temperatures inside the refrigerator compartment are kept between 35° and 40°; temperatures inside the freezer should be near 0°. You can test the refrigerator compartment's temperature by keeping a thermometer inside half a glass of water on a shelf for 8 hours, or by doing the "milk test." Put a milk carton on the top shelf and check it a day later; if it is too warm or too cold, adjust the controls. You can test the freezer compartment by putting a thermometer between 2 packages of frozen food overnight, or by using the "ice cream" test. Put the ice cream in the center of the freezer compartment and check it after a day. If it's too hard or too soft, adjust the controls. Premium ice creams with a high cream content normally require slightly lower temperatures than the more "airy" brands that have a low cream content.

(**Note:** If the temperatures in your home drop below 60° at night, it may cause the compressor to operate less often, allowing the freezer compartment to warm somewhat. You may want to adjust the freezer control so that it is 1 setting colder to protect frozen food—especially when the thermostat is turned down for an extended period. If freezing occurs in the fresh food compartment, adjust the control so that it is 1 step warmer for that side.)

Helpful hint: Unplug the refrigerator before making any repairs. Also unplug it even if you are only replacing a burned-out light bulb. A light bulb may break when being replaced; unplugging the unit allows you to avoid any contact with a live wire filament. Note that turning controls to the "off" position does

not cut off the power to the light circuit.

• • •

71 Microwave Doesn't Work

Problem: Microwave won't operate, or takes longer to cook food than times suggested in cookbooks.

Background: Microwaves are like radio or radar waves. They will pass through glass, plastic, paper and most other containers that are not of metal. Microwaves bounce off of metal and are absorbed by food. When food absorbs microwaves, heat is created because water molecules in the food bounce around, colliding with each other. Heat is created by these collisions, much like the way your hands warm when you rub them together. For minor problems, which you can solve yourself, see the following suggestions. For other problems, check your owner's manual or call a service technician.

What to do: If the microwave will not operate, make sure the unit is plugged in. If it's plugged in and still doesn't work, the cause may be faulty wiring, a blown fuse, or a tripped circuit breaker. Check to see whether the oven door is securely closed and that the controls are set correctly. Also check the air vents to make sure they are not blocked. The oven may overheat and turn off if the air vents are blocked. Let the oven cool for an hour, then restart it. If it still won't operate, call a service technician.

If it takes the microwave longer than it should to cook food, check with your local utility company to see if the voltage in your area is fluctuating below the normal operating range. Next check to see if the microwave is operating on the same electrical circuit as another appliance. If so, the cooking times will increase when both of the units are on at the same time. (Note: It's best if the microwave does not share a circuit with any other appliance.) If the unit has a glass shelf, check to see that it is in place. If it isn't, cooking times may be affected. Cooking time will also increase if more or larger amounts of food are placed in the oven than a recipe calls for, if the food is frozen or was refrigerated immediately before being put in the oven. (Some recipes reflect the time needed to cook food that is at room temperature.)

Special advice: Microwaves should not be adjusted or repaired by anyone except properly qualified service technicians. After a repair is made, the technician should check for microwave leakage. To avoid potentially harmful exposure to microwave energy, don't attempt to operate the microwave with the door open. Don't tamper with safety interlocks. Don't put any object between the oven front face and the door, or allow soil or cleaner residue to accumulate on sealing surfaces. Also, don't operate the microwave if the door doesn't close properly, if it is bent, if its hinges or latches are broken or loose, or if its seals or sealing surfaces are damaged.

Helpful hint: Remove metal ties from plastic bags before placing bags in the oven and check carry-out food for metal before reheating. For cooking times longer than 4 minutes, avoid using paper containers which may burn, and be careful when using plastics because some may melt. Don't attempt to cook eggs in the shell because steam buildup inside may cause them to burst.

● ● ●

72 Portable Humidifier Malfunctions

Problem: Portable, belt-type humidifier doesn't run, or continues to run for extended periods.

Background: Portable humidifiers, which use wide belts of porous material partially submerged in a tank reservoir to evaporate moisture into the room, usually will have a variable speed control (controlling how fast the belt turns) as well as an automatic humidity control. Some units have colored pilot lights; one which signals when the cord is plugged in and the variable speed control is in the operational range, and another which signals when the unit has shut down automatically because the water level in the reservoir has gotten too low.

What to do: If the unit does not run, make sure it is plugged in to a live outlet. If it does not turn on, it may be because the humidistat is set below the relative humidity of the room, or because the humidistat has not had enough time to adjust to the conditions in the home (this may take several hours). If the home and furnishings are exceptionally dry, the humidifier may operate for an extended period of time. After proper humidity is reached, the operation time of the unit will be shorter. If the humidifier continues to run excessively, check for open doors or windows, as well as for an open fireplace damper. The air escaping up the chimney can cause 2 or more complete air changes in the home per hour; the more air changes, the greater the humidity requirements.

Special advice: For the most effective humidification, keep doors open to all rooms to be humidified. Do not place the unit with its back grille too near drapes or curtains. Air movement could pull drapes against the grille and cut off air flow, resulting in possible damage to the humidifier or the drapes. For maximum efficiency, the evaporator belt should be replaced at least

once a season, or more often under severe conditions. The unit should be cleaned periodically, and emptied and cleaned at the end of the season. Also, once a season, put 2 to 4 drops of oil in any oiling tubes provided on the fan motor.

Helpful hint: All humidifiers containing water for extended periods will eventually develop odors. Periodic cleaning, and the use of water treatment tables, can help prevent this. For very persistent odors, use 2 tablespoons of chlorine bleach diluted in 1 gallon of water to clean the tank and the evaporator belt.

●●●

73 Portable Dehumidifier Defective

Problem: Dehumidifier freezes up or does not seem to be working.

Background: Smaller, portable dehumidifiers are much like air conditioners in that they have a fan, a fan motor, and a refrigerant system. Like an air conditioner, regular care and maintenance can help prevent operational problems. Once a year the refrigerant coils should be cleaned with a rag, brush, or vacuum cleaner. If the unit does not have an oil-less fan motor it should be oiled once a year with a few drops of oil in each of the oil holes. (Note: It's likely the cabinet will need to be removed to clean the coils or to oil the fan motor.)

What to do: Dehumidifiers rely on an automatic humidistat to turn the unit on and off to maintain the humidity level you select (usually 60% to 65% when set in the "normal" range). If the unit stops running, first check the power cord to see that it is plugged in properly and be sure that the outlet is receiving power. If not, check the main power panel for a blown fuse or a tripped circuit breaker. Use a different outlet, if necessary, to avoid overloading a circuit. Dehumidifiers can become blocked with ice in temperatures below 65°. Most units are not designed to operate below that temperature, and in most cases dehumidification is not needed below 70°; shut off the unit until the room temperature rises.

Special advice: Once the humidistat control is set, the unit will shut off when the relative humidity reaches that level. It will turn on again automatically when the humidity rises. Note: The compressor may stop if you turn off the dehumidifier, and immediately turn it on again. This is normal. In about 2 minutes the compressor should start up again automatically and continue to run.

Helpful hint: If you use the unit on a sloping floor, make sure the drain hole is located on the downgrade slope. Also do not block either end of the unit, because it takes air from the front and exhausts it through the back. To clean the exterior cabinet parts, use warm sudsy water, rinse with clear water, and do not turn on the unit until the exterior is completely dry.

•••

74 Sink Disposal Jammed Up

Problem: Sink disposal becomes jammed because of material dropped into it which cannot be ground up.

Background: Most in-sink disposals are faithful servants, but occasionally some become jammed by foreign objects accidentally dropped into them, or by highly fibrous waste, such as corn husks, lima bean pods, or artichoke leaves. Usually most vegetable and table scraps are no problem, but whole rinds, grapefruit skins, or corn cobs should be cut into smaller pieces before being

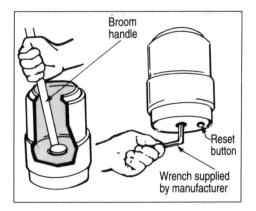

fed into the disposal. Disposals are not intended to grind items made of glass, metal, leather, cloth, rubber, string, feathers, plastic, or paper.

What to do: Clearing a sink disposal is usually easy; however, be careful to avoid personal injury or causing damage to the unit. To free a jam, turn off water and turn the disposal power switch to "off." Then remove as much food waste as possible using a pair of long-handled tongs or pliers. Many manufacturers supply a small wrench to clear jams. Insert one end of wrench into the hole underneath the unit, and work it back and forth until it moves freely for at least one complete turn. Remove the wrench, wait 5 minutes to let the disposal motor cool, then press the reset button at the bottom of the unit. Turn on the water and the disposal and let them run until all debris has been thoroughly flushed out.

If your unit does not have a wrench, or if you can't find yours (wrenches are best kept taped to a pipe near the disposal under the sink), then try using a broom handle or something similar. Remove excess material with tongs. Then push the broom handle down inside the disposal so it contacts with the grinding blades. Work the flywheel (the moving mechanism you see when looking down into the disposal) back and forth, remove any additional material, and press the reset button. Turn on the water and the disposal.

Special advice: Do not put your fingers or hands in the disposal at any time. To avoid possible injury which may be caused by the unit expelling hazardous material, do not use it to grind clam or oyster shells, glass, china, plastic, large whole bones, or any metal. Don't put chemical drain cleaners or lye into the disposal. A spoon, bottle cap, or other foreign object dropped into the unit will probably make loud, unusual noises. To clear, turn off the disposal and the water, remove the object, and continue grinding.

Helpful hint: If the motor does not restart, make sure you have pushed the reset button. If it still doesn't work, check for blown fuses or tripped circuit breakers. If a unit without a reset button won't start, the overload protector may be defective and the motor may have to be replaced.

●●●

75 Phone Doesn't Work

Problem: Phone doesn't operate, emits excessive noise or rapid busy signal.

Background: Problems can stem from your phone set, the wiring inside your home, or in outside lines and switching equipment. A rapid busy signal means all phone circuits are busy; try your call again in a few minutes. Noise on phone may be caused by weather, aerial satellites, poor grounding, or other temporary conditions. (If the noise persists, the tips below may help you identify the problem.) Interference may also come from citizens band (CB) radios and AM/FM broadcast stations. Installing a modular filter, available through stores that sell phone equipment, may help. Cordless phones (see entry 76) use radio frequencies and may receive interference from radio transmitters. If so, contact the cordless phone supplier or manufacturer for help.

What to do: First make sure all phones are hung up. If you have only one phone, take it to another home and plug it in. If it doesn't work there, the problem is likely in the phone. If you have two or more phones, unplug them all. Then try each one—one at a time—in each phone jack. If a phone doesn't work anywhere, the problem is most likely in that phone. If none work in one jack, the problem is with the jack. You might also borrow a friend's phone and try it in each of your jacks. If it doesn't work in one jack, that jack is the problem. If it doesn't work in any jack, the problem may be in the line.

(Note: If you have installed new phone wire or jacks, you can test the installation by plugging a phone into the jack and listening for a dial tone. You should be able to interrupt the dial tone by dialing any single number other than 0. If the dial tone is not interrupted, reverse the wires at the jack. If you still don't hear a dial tone, recheck the connections and equipment.)

Special advice: If there is no dial tone, make sure the line cord is firmly plugged into the jack and phone, and that the handset cord is firmly plugged in at both ends. If the phone won't ring, check to see that the ringer switch is set to "on." If so, note the ringer equivalence number (REN) on the bottom and ask your phone company if it requires more ringing power than is normal. If there is static, check for a loose handset cord or, if possible, try another cord. (Some weather conditions, such as very low humidity, can cause static buildup.) If you get a dial tone, but can't dial out, make sure the tone/pulse switch is set to "pulse" if you have rotary-only service.

Helpful hint: If you have phone accessories—such as answering machines, speaker phones, or cordless phones—make sure they are working. If phones work without the added equipment, the problem may be with the accessories. If you have a phone connected to an answering machine and have a dial tone but can't dial out, try plugging only the phone into the jack. If it works, you may have a compatibility problem and may need a 2-for-1 adaptor, available where phone equipment is sold.

•••

76 Cordless Phone Defective

Problem: Cordless phone doesn't work at all, or has static, noise, or a weak signal.

Background: Cordless phones, which provide walk-about convenience, depend on radio signals to transmit between the handset and base unit, using batteries in the handset and an AC power supply to the base. They must be plugged into both a telephone jack and an electrical outlet. Some may have more than one channel which can be used to transmit. A cordless phone's performance depends on several factors, such as the distance between the handset and base unit, the home's building materials, and the weather. They work best when antennas are completely pulled out and, in a multilevel home, when used in a room on an upper floor.

What to do: If you just installed the phone and it doesn't work, make sure the power cord is plugged in, that the cord between the wall jack and base unit is firmly connected, and that the antennas are pulled out. If the phone beeps when you press the "phone" button, or if the phone indicator light (on the handset) doesn't come on when you press "phone," the batteries may need recharging. If you recently replaced batteries, double-check to be sure they are correctly installed.

If you get static, noise, or a weak signal (even when you are close to the base), pull the antenna out fully and change channels if the phone has more than one channel. Noise can be caused by household appliances or other cordless phones. If possible, plug the base AC cord into another electrical outlet, which is not on the same circuit as other appliances. Also try moving the base to a higher location, such as a second or third floor.

If the phone doesn't ring on incoming calls, make sure the ringer switch on the base is set to "on," pull out the antenna, and move closer to the base or unplug some other phones; you may have too many phones to allow them all to ring audibly. If you hear other calls on the line, change channels if possible. Or disconnect the phone and connect a conventional phone. If you still hear other calls, the problem is likely in your wiring or the phone company's lines. If you hear a lot of noise and none of the phone's features work, try hanging up for a few seconds to make sure the handset and base are operating on the same channel and security code.

Special advice: If you walk out of range without pressing "off," a cordless phone may be left off the hook. To hang it up properly, walk back into range, and periodically press "off" until the "phone" indicator light goes out. Instead of pressing the switchhook (as you would with a conventional phone) to signal phone company equipment for services like call waiting, briefly press the "phone" button.

Helpful hint: Don't depend on a cordless phone as the only phone in your home; it is best used as a second phone. A cordless phone will not operate in the event of a power failure, while conventional phones don't rely on AC power and thus should work.

• • •

77 Steam Iron Works Poorly

Problem: Clogged spray openings, clogged steam vents, or sputtering prevent proper operation.

Background: Lint can collect in an iron's steam vents and spray openings, and steam vents can become quickly clogged with minerals in your tap water. Sputtering may occur if the water storage tank has been filled to the overflow vent; if the thermostat setting is too low, al-lowing water to run through without being turned into steam; or if the setting is too high, causing the water to flow through the steam passages so fast that it comes out as drops.

What to do: Using distilled or de-mineralized water helps keep spray openings and steam vents from clogging. Most manufacturer's instructions discourage the use of steam iron cleaners. To clean slightly clogged vents, use a mixture of equal parts of distilled white vinegar and distilled water. Then fill the water chamber and set the iron on the rayon setting for a half hour. Cool the iron and then flush it through with distilled water. Some irons can be taken apart for cleaning. On other models, lint and loose mineral deposits are automatically flushed out with bursts of steam.

Special advice: Although you should avoid using tap water in steam irons, a new iron can be seasoned by using tap water for the first 4 or 5 ironings. Minerals in the tap water will lightly coat the metal and prevent distilled or demineralized water from etching the metal.

Helpful hint: The bottom of the iron (soleplate) can be cleaned with detergent and water, baking soda, whiting, a soap-filled steel wool pad, or fine-grade sandpaper. After cleaning the iron, run waxed paper over it and polish it with a cloth.

• • •

78 Electric Blanket Doesn't Work

Problem: Electric blanket doesn't seem to be heating properly.

Background: Electric blankets that are not operating should be returned to the store from which they were purchased. Often, however, they may not operate properly because something is interfering with the control's ability to gauge the room temperature and properly control the blanket's warmth.

What to do: To troubleshoot with an electric blanket, first check the outlet and all connections. Be sure the wired portion of the blanket is not tucked in under the mattress or bed slat, and that it is not crimped against the wall or footboard. This will cause the safety thermostats to shut off. The blanket also may not operate if the average room temperature is much above 72°. Check to be sure the control is not covered by another blanket, sheet, or spread. Also while in use, avoid laying books or heavy items on the blanket, don't sit on it, and don't cover it with another blanket or bedspread.

Special advice: To test an electric blanket to see if it is operating, fold the blanket, connect the control, and plug it into the outlet. Turn the control to high and wait 10 minutes. You should be able to feel its warmth when you put your hand between the folds.

Helpful hint: Avoid folding the blanket when it is in use, do not use it for infants, disabled persons, or anyone sensitive to heat. Always turn an electric blanket off when not in use. Also, if a dual-control blanket doesn't seem to work, check to make sure it is not turned over, causing the control on one side to operate the blanket on the opposite side, and vice versa.

HOME INTERIORS

● ● ● ● ● ● ● ● ● ● ● ● ●

79 Water in Basement

Problem: Groundwater or rain-water seeps or floods into basement.

Background: Water problems in cellars or basements is a common problem which may have a single cause or a number of causes. For example, the home may have settled over the years, the grading around the home may not have been done properly, or the exterior of the basement walls below the grade may not have been properly waterproofed before backfilling. In certain cases, the basement may be only inches above the groundwater level, may be positioned in the path of normal underground runoff, or may be sunk into heavy clay which interferes with normal drainage. Much-improved drain-tile systems (underground drain systems around the perimeter of the house, often connected to a sump pump) and a waterproof membrane are installed in newer homes before the basement slab is poured.

What to do: Basement moisture problems occur in the form of condensation, seepage, or leakage. Of these, the seepage of small or moderate amounts of water often can be easily corrected at a low cost. The causes can include soil becoming saturated around the home because of roof runoff; grading, which slopes toward the home; rainwater collecting in window wells; or excessive watering along the foundation wall. Make some observations, especially during rain storms. If the grade around the home (including planting beds) slopes toward the home, correct it so it slopes away from the walls. If window wells have sunk, build them up and fill the cracks or crevices around them. Correct leaking or improperly sloped roof gutters; if your roof does not have gutters, consider installing them. If needed, install downspout leaders, splash blocks, or both, so roof water discharges at least 3 feet away from the foundation. Check adjacent areas, such as driveways, walks, and patios to make sure they drain away from the home.

Special advice: If seepage occurs under little or no pressure, applying 2 coats of a waterproofing paint or compound may help. If a test area is successful after several weeks, cover the entire problem area. If water is seeping through holes or cracks ⅛ inch or larger, clean them out and patch them with hydraulic cement, which sets fast and expands when wet. (Prepare larger cracks or holes using a dovetail groove, which is wider toward the back of the opening than the front.) If seepage is under pressure, a solution is used to install a weep pipe near the floor-wall joint where the pressure is greatest, using a masonry drill or a star chisel (use striking hammer and proper safety gear). If water continues to discharge through the pipe, leave it in and direct the discharge to a drain or a sump pump with a hose.

Helpful hint: In cases where seepage under pressure occurs at the wall-floor joint, 3 options exist. For light seepage, try sealing the joint with 2 coats of a waterproofing compound. For moderate seepage, chisel out a 2-inch wide, 1-inch thick dovetail groove. Clean out and use a mix of hydraulic or mortar cement to build an inverted cove-shaped patch. When heavy seepage develops, a solution may be to install several weep pipes which discharge excess moisture through hoses, concrete troughs, or commercial devices, to a sump pump or drain. If

large amounts of water regularly enter the basement, major corrective action may be necessary. Contact a reputable contractor for advice.

● ● ●

80 Tub-Wall Seal Leaks

Problem: Grout or seal around top tub edges deteriorates, allowing water to leak through the joint.

Background: The crack between the bathtub and wall should always be tightly sealed, because moisture can damage the walls, the ceilings below the bathroom, and the house frame. Besides waterproof grout, several types of sealer are available, including press-in-place caulk, and latex caulking compounds. Hardware stores and home centers will have a variety of products to choose from.

What to do: The first step is to scrape away the old grout or sealer from the joint areas using the pointed end of an old-type can opener or another available tool. Wash the surface to remove soap, grease, and dirt, then dry before applying new material. If using waterproof grout, slowly add water and mix until a thick paste forms, then press the mixture into the crack with a putty knife. Wipe off excess grout before it dries, and let it dry thoroughly before using

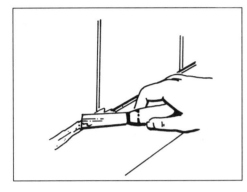

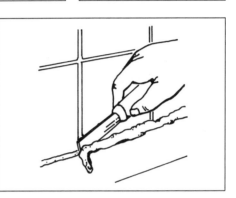

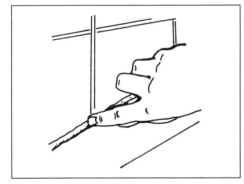

the tub. If using newer products, such as latex caulking compound, fill the area at a 45° bevel and smoothen it with a small tool such as an old spoon, putty knife, or spatula.

Special advice: Double-check the instructions on a product's label before you buy it. Sealers that come in a tube can be squeezed in a ribbon along the crack. Because some products dry quickly, be prepared to work quite fast if you want to end up with a neat-looking job. If you are using grout, discard any leftover mixture (do not put it down the drain) and wash any containers or tools before the grout dries on them.

Helpful hint: One way to do a neater job is to line the edges of the crack to be filled with masking tape, and then remove it after the job is completed. However, prepackaged, press-in-place caulk ribbons are easy to install and are worth the extra money if you want professional-looking results.

•••

81 Tile Wall Is Crumbling

Problem: A section of tile on bathroom wall becomes loose and begins to fall out.

Background: Loose tile, especially in tub areas, should be taken care of as soon as possible. If loose tiles are neglected, water can get in behind them and cause the entire wall to disintegrate. When replacing sections of tile, be sure to examine the surface underneath. If damage is extensive because of moisture, it may need to be replaced with water-resistant gypsum backing board before re-tiling. Bathroom tile that is in good shape can generally be reused if the existing adhesive is removed.

What to do: Remove loose or damaged tile. If the grout used for ceramic tile is ⅛ inch wide or less, dig it out with an old-style can opener or a similar tool. With ceramic tile, use a centerpunch and hammer to punch a hole through the tile's center, and use a glass cutter to score an "X." Break out the tile in pieces, with hammer and cold chisel, starting from the center. (Try not to damage the wall surface underneath.) Clean out the opening. Plastic tiles can be loosened with a heat gun or hair dryer.

Use waterproof adhesive and coat the back of the new tile to within half an inch of the edges on all sides, using a putty knife. Hold

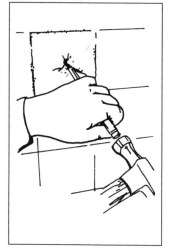

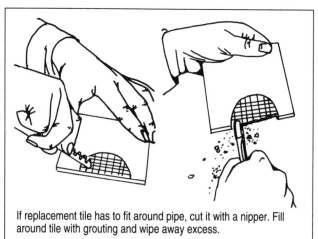

If replacement tile has to fit around pipe, cut it with a nipper. Fill around tile with grouting and wipe away excess.

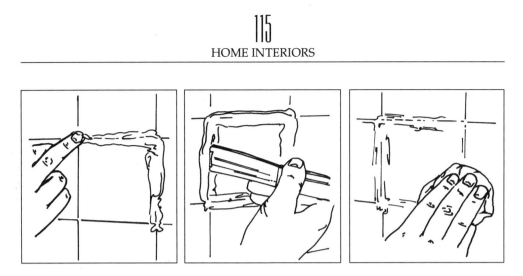

the tile by the edges and position it so it is in line with the surrounding tiles. For ceramic tile, wait 24 hours before applying any premixed grouting cement around the tile. Wet the tile edges and fill all the spaces around the tile with grouting, pressing it into the joints with a sponge. After about an hour, remove the excess grouting, which will be dry and brittle. If the grouting is not smooth or has gaps, wet the tile edges again and repeat the process.

Special advice: If you need to replace ceramic tile around pipes, corners, and other difficult-to-fit areas, use the old tile as a pattern. If you can't, then use a cardboard template to mark the area to be cut out with a tile nipper. Another method is to use a glass cutter to score the outline of the part to be removed, then score crisscross lines over the part and use a pair of pliers to break off a small square at a time. File the edge smooth before positioning the tile to the wall.

Helpful hint: If you are replacing plastic tile, it will be less apt to break if it is warmed first. Toothpicks may be helpful in positioning the new tile. To remove any adhesive that may have gotten onto the tiles, use a small cloth dipped in paint thinner or any other solvent specified on the container. Use a wet sponge to remove any remaining grout.

● ● ●

82 Window Glass Is Broken

Problem: Glass pane in window is broken, cracked, or scarred.

Background: Most local hardware stores offer glass replacement services and can replace glass in wooden double-sash windows, horizontal sliding windows, casement windows, wood or aluminum storm windows or doors, or awning or jalousie windows. If you plan to replace the glass in a wooden window yourself, assemble a hammer, screwdriver, putty knife, and measuring rule or tape. Then add a small

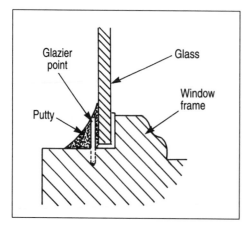

package of glazier's points, window putty, and either a soldering iron or a small propane torch to your supplies. (If you don't have these materials, pick them up where you have your new glass cut.)

What to do: First remove the old putty, softening the old putty with either a soldering iron, small pro-

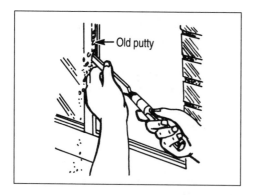

pane torch, or heat gun. Heat makes even ancient putty pliable and easy to remove. If you don't want to invest in any of these tools, you might get by with an old clothes iron, or by soaking older oil-based putty with linseed oil to soften it.

Under the putty you'll see small triangular glazier points used to hold the pane in place. Pry these points out with a screwdriver and remove the old glass. (Wear gloves and goggles to avoid accidental injury.)

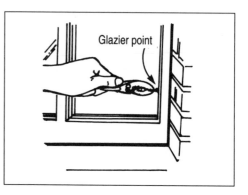

Cutting your own glass to fit from larger sheets saves some money, but it does take practice to become accurate and avoid breakage. However, if you do cut your own glass, panes for most wooden windows should be cut ⅛ inch smaller than the opening, both in length and height. Cut panes for vertical-sash aluminum storm windows 1/32 inch smaller than the opening.

Clean and sand the groove for the pane. If you are using oil-based glazing compound, apply a coat of linseed oil or thinned exterior paint around the groove. This keeps the window from absorbing oil from the compound. Then apply a thin layer of compound (just enough to act as a seal), and insert the pane. Fasten it in place with glazier's points every 4 inches to 6 inches around the opening. Use a hammer and putty knife

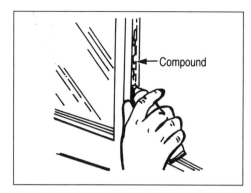

Compound

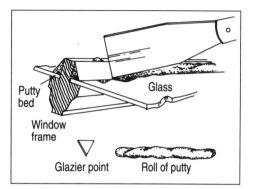

Putty bed

Glass

Window frame

Glazier point   Roll of putty

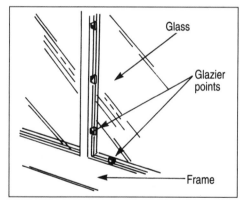

Glass

Glazier points

Frame

Simply dab it in place and smooth it down with your putty knife. You can paint over this type of putty in 30 minutes or so; with oil-based compound let it cure for a week or more before painting. Use exterior paint and make sure the paint touches the glass. This prevents cracks that can trap moisture from occurring.

Special advice: When buying replacement glass, you will have a choice of single- or double-strength glass. If the pane is 12 inches × 16 inches or smaller, you can use single-strength; if it is larger, buy the more expensive double-strength.

Helpful hint: Putting linseed oil on the putty knife can help you do a smooth, professional-looking job with oil-based putty. If you are using newer acrylic-latex putty, putting water on the knife will help lubricate it. If you are using oil-based putty that is old and hard, put it in a glass container and microwave it for a short time to make it more pliable and easier to work with.

or screwdriver to drive them halfway into the wood.

If you are using oil-based compound, roll it into a rope about ½ inch in diameter, press it in place, and smoothen with a putty knife held at an angle. If you are using newer acrylic latex glazing compound, do not precoat the groove.

• • •

83 Window Frame Is Stuck

Problem: Window won't open because of paint, dirt, or moisture problems.

Background: Though windows can become stuck in periods of high humidity, they often stick because they are painted shut. Windows may also stick because their channels or guides need cleaning and/or lubricating.

What to do: If the window is stuck because it has been painted shut, use a utility knife and insert it between the window stop and the sash (wood part of the window). Slide it along the crack all the way around the window. Local hardware stores or home centers may carry other tools designed for this purpose; one is called a window zipper. Next, if the window still appears to be stuck, use a short piece of scrap lumber, such as a 2×2, and place it against the sash. Tap lightly on the scrap wood with a hammer.

Special advice: To free the window you may have to take out the window stops by removing any visible screws. If the stops are nailed, use a thin pry bar to remove them, working close to the nail locations. After removing the stops, sand or lightly plane them so the window will move freely.

Helpful hint: When painting or repainting windows, make sure you move the window once or twice while the paint is drying to prevent the stuck-window syndrome.

● ● ●

84 Drawer Is Stuck

Problem: Drawer is hard to open, sticks occasionally, or can't be opened.

Background: Old-style drawers which slide on wood often can be fixed to move more easily. New-style drawers may slide on tracks inside the drawer cavity where sticking may be caused by worn-out tracks or rollers.

What to do: For drawers that ride on wooden guides, remove the drawer and look for shiny spots on the top or bottom edges of the drawer, or on the sides. Sand these shiny areas, then try the drawer again to see if it moves more easily. Repeat the sanding if it still sticks, and then rub the drawer bottom and the drawer frame where they contact with candle wax, paraffin, or soap. This will make drawers, especially those filled with heavy items, glide easier.

Special advice: If the glides are badly worn, the drawer may not close all the way, and the drawer front may strike the frame. In this case, the drawer needs to be lifted. Remove it and insert 2 or 3 large smooth-headed thumbtacks along the front of each glide. If the drawer sticks because of damp weather and only opens partially, drying it with a hair dryer may work (be careful not to start a fire). If the drawer won't open any other way, it may be necessary to remove the back, if accessible.

Helpful hint: If you find that drawers are sticking only in damp weather, wait until the weather is dry and the drawers are not sticking. Then coat the unfinished wood with a penetrating sealer or with wax.

• • •

85 Defects in Wallpaper

Problem: Wallpaper loosens at edges, becomes ripped, or creates bubbles.

Background: Even newer wall coverings, though much improved, can become damaged. Blisters in wallpaper can be fixed by lancing the wallpaper with a razor blade or a craft knife to let the air out, then putting glue behind the loose paper and smoothening it with a wet sponge. Loose edges can simply be reglued with wallpaper adhesive. Rips and tears, however, require more work but can be repaired if the damaged area is not too large and you have extra wallpaper.

What to do: With ripped or torn wallpaper, you can often create an almost invisible patch. Find a section of extra wallpaper larger than the damaged area, and tape it over the damaged area, matching the pattern. Using a razor blade, craft knife, or utility knife, cut straight lines (in the shape of a square, rectangle, triangle) through both the new patch paper and the wallpaper on the wall. Next remove the top patch paper, as well as the paper on the wall, within the cut area. Coat the back of the patch with wallpaper adhesive, and fit it into the hole. Smoothen and wipe the patch with a damp sponge.

Special advice: If a bubble is next to an edge, you may be able to get rid of it by lifting the edge with a knife. Another way to flatten bubbles is to inject glue behind the bubbled paper with a needle-type injector which resembles a hypodermic needle. If wallpaper that isn't washable becomes smudged, check a local wallpaper store for special wallpaper dough or gum erasers to clean it with.

Helpful hint: Often extra leftover wallpaper, after a few years, will look newer and brighter than wallpaper on the wall. To age patch material (so it will match), keep it exposed to similar conditions in an out-of-the-way place.

• • •

86 Hole in Wallboard

Problem: Damage has resulted in a hole in a wall or ceiling that is made of gypsum board.

Background: Small- to medium-sized holes can be mended with joint compound (either ready-mix or powder which is mixed with water) or with products called patching plaster or spackling compounds. Large holes may require cutting the wallboard back to the studs, and replacing the entire damaged section. For tips on repairing plaster walls or ceilings, see entry 88. For repairing cracks or nail pops in gypsum board, see entry 87.

Back paper

Front paper

What to do: One way to fix a smaller hole is to use a plug method. With this technique, first mark a neat rectangle around the damaged area and use a utility knife or keyhole saw to cut out the area. Mark the hole's dimensions on a scrap piece of gypsum board, which is at least 2 inches larger all the way around. Make another outline 2 inches around the plug area, then cut through this line completely. Next cut on the border of the plug, without cutting through the bottom paper layer. Peel off the gypsum board material in this 2-inch ring around the plug, leaving the full-sized paper intact around the plug's perimeter. Spread patching compound around both the opening and the edges of the hole.

Press the plug firmly in place, hold a few minutes until the patch has set, then apply compound over the entire area.

Another method is to fill smaller holes with crumpled newspaper and patch them with joint compound or patching plaster. A third method is

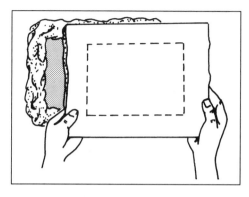

to use a piece of string and a rectangular piece of gypsum board slightly larger than the hole. Put string through the center with the knot in the back and cover the patch's outside edges with compound or construction adhesive. Push the patch inside hole, pull on

the string to bring the patch against the back of the original wall or ceiling and hold it in place until it sets. Then fill in the area with joint compound.

Special advice: Another method, similar to the one above, is to insert a section of wallboard longer than the hole, and fasten it in place with sheetrock screws. With all methods,

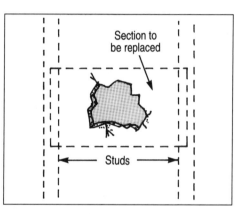

apply patching compound over the entire area, smoothening the material and compound beyond the edges of the damage. Feather the edges so the patch is flush with the wall surface. Remove excess compound and let the patch dry. Reapply more compound if shrinkage occurs, then sand, prime, and paint.

Helpful hint: Patching plaster and spackling compounds are extremely porous and must be primed before painting. In some cases a coat of paint can be used as a primer before a second (final) coat is applied. Check the paint's label to see if it is recommended as a primer. Allow

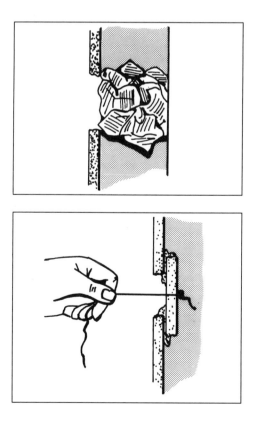

primers adequate drying time before applying final paint.

• • •

87 Defects in Wallboard

Problem: Nails pop out of wallboard, or unsightly cracks develop.

Background: Poor materials or original construction technique, changes in temperature, and other problems can cause nail pops or cracks. Cracks often occur in newly constructed homes as the home settles. Some cracks can be annoyingly persistent; however, first try to fix them using the tips below. If that doesn't work, check with suppliers for special products such as fiberglass tape designed for hard-to-fix cracks. For tips on handling holes in gypsum board walls or ceilings, see entry 86. For fixing holes in plaster, see entry 88.

What to do: To fix popped nail heads, first reinforce the area with additional fasteners (nails or screws), driving them about 1 inch to 1½ inches above and below the popped heads. Push the wallboard toward the stud or rafter as you drive the nail in. If using nails, drive slightly into the surface to form a dimple that holds new patching material. Let patching dry overnight and reapply if shrinkage occurs.

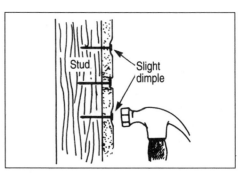

When patch is completely dry, sand lightly and finish.

To fix narrow cracks, use a stiff brush or screwdriver to remove loose material from the crack. Bend the point of a can opener or similar object into a hook and use it to enlarge and undercut the crack opening so it will provide a secure hold for the patching compound. (Dampen edges of crack when using patching compound mixed with water.) Fill

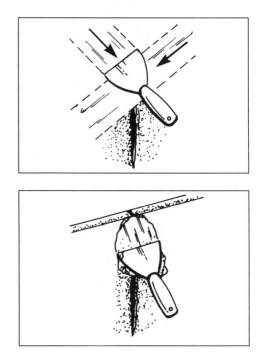

deep cracks almost to the surface with compound. Let dry, then add another thin coat. Smoothen it on each side by feathering it about 2 inches. Let it dry and sand it smooth.

Special advice: Deep, wide cracks stay patched longer when reinforced with joint tape. Use perforated drywall tape and patching compound. Sand 6 inches on each side of the crack and work the patching material down into the crack. Then center the tape over the crack, pressing it down with a wide drywall knife. Cover the tape with a coat of the material, smoothing it well beyond the tape edges by feathering. Let the patch dry overnight, then apply another coat extending 1 inch to 1½ inches beyond the edges of last coat. Smooth, let dry, and lightly sand.

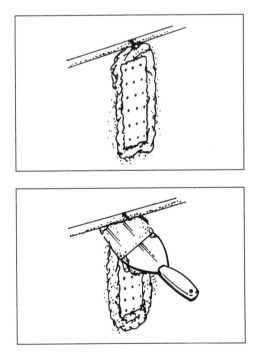

Helpful hint: To make the patch's edges even with the surface of the wallboard, use feathering strokes when applying patching compound. Make small, successive overlapping X-like strokes across the area, working from the top of the patch to the bottom. Start and end each stroke on an area of clean wall outside of the patch area.

●●●

88 Hole or Crack in Plaster

Problem: A hole or crack in plaster walls or ceiling needs repair.

Background: Two types of patching compounds are available: 1) spackling compound which is convenient for small jobs and can be bought as powder or ready mixed, and 2) patching plaster which can be bought in larger packages and needs to be mixed with water. For repairing holes or cracks in the wallboard, see entry 87.

What to do: Both small cracks and holes can be filled with patching mixture; large holes may need to be filled step-by-step. First remove any loose plaster. Then use a knife to scrape out the plaster from the back of the crack so that the back is wider than the front surface. Thoroughly

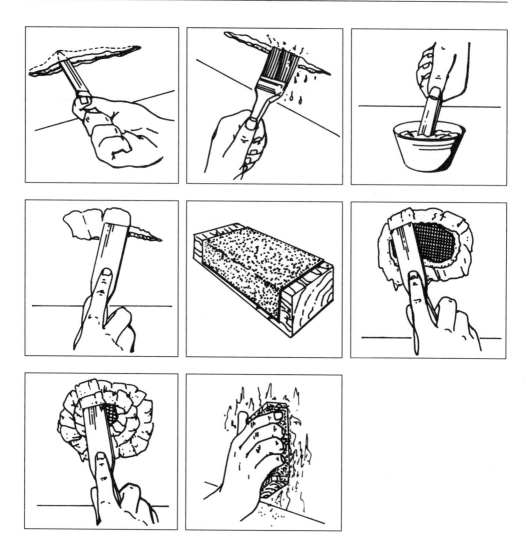

dampen the surface of the crack with a wet cloth or paint brush, mix up a small amount of patching compound and fill in the crack with it. Smoothen the surface with a putty knife and sand the patch area after it has dried.

For larger holes or cracks, fill the hole partially and allow it to dry as a base for a final fill. Then add a second batch of compound. Let dry and sand until smooth. For large holes,

you may need to fill in the area behind the crack with wadded newspaper. Begin patching by working inward from all sides. Let dry, then apply another layer around the new edge. Repeat until the hole is filled. Allow to dry and sand smooth.

Special advice: If the surface beyond the repair is textured, you can attempt to match the surface of the patch while the plaster is still wet. A sponge, comb, or other device can be used to accomplish the texturing.

Helpful hint: To sand repaired areas, it can be helpful to wrap sandpaper around a small length of wood. This will help keep the surface even. To check for ridges, hold a trouble-light or lamp next to the wall on one side or the other.

●●●

89 Furniture Finish Damaged

Problem: Furniture has been blemished with water spots or rings, burn marks from ciga-rettes, or minor scratches.

Background: Almost any furniture that is used regularly suffers an oc-casional nick, scratch, burn, or water spot. Though a number of commer-cial products are available to correct minor defects, furniture-finish ex-pert Homer Formby suggests many alternative home remedies, many which use products you probably al-ready have in the house.

What to do: To treat water spots and rings caused by moisture trapped underneath wax, try applying tooth-paste. Squeeze it onto a wet cotton rag and buff the spotted area. For stubborn areas, combine toothpaste in equal parts with baking soda, an-other gentle abrasive. Buff until the spot disappears. Then with a clean cloth continue buffing until you can see yourself. For burn marks, such as those caused by cigarettes, try using nail polish remover. Dip a cotton swab into the remover and rub it lightly across the burn mark. This dissolves the black residue. If any burn mark remains, scrape it gently with a small knife. If a slight hollow remains, mix equal parts remover with clear nail polish and apply 1 coat at a time with the nail polish brush. Let each coat dry between ap-plications (it might take up to 8 coats or so).

Special advice: For minor scratches or other mars on furniture, try using a color crayon which matches the finish. Melt the crayon over the scratch until it flows over the mar, let it cure for half an hour, then gently shave off the residue with a credit card. You can melt the crayon with a soldering iron. Or if you don't have a soldering iron, tie a nail to a pencil, heat it over a flame, then put the nail to the crayon.

Helpful hint: To mask the musty odor in antique furniture, you can use red cedar shavings (not western cedar). Put the shavings in the toe of an old pair of nylons, tie the end, and cut off the excess. Then tack the sack along the back of the drawer or, if there are no drawers, on the back of the furniture or underneath it.

●●●

90 Floors or Stairs Squeak

Problem: Floors or stairs emit annoying squeaks when stepped on.

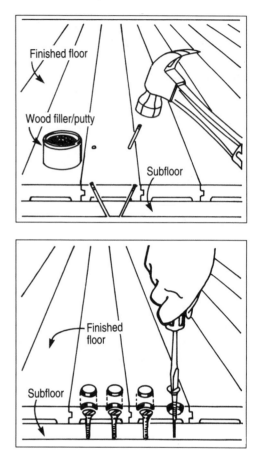

Background: Floor or stair squeaks are common in homes and are usually caused by floor components rubbing against each other. Squeaks can be caused by floor materials that have dried out and become loose or separated. They may also be caused by loose X-bridging between the joists, by gaps between the joists and subflooring, or by plumbing pipes or ducts rubbing against the joists.

What to do: First try to pinpoint the area of the squeak and see if the problem can be fixed from below the floor or stairs. Check to see if the squeak may be caused by the X-bridging lumber, which is used between the joists visible in the basement. You may be able to correct this by cutting away wood where the Xs cross with a handsaw. Check and readjust any loose pipes or pipe hangers in that area. If there is a gap between the joist and subflooring, try driving in wedge-shaped shims above the joist. The squeak may be caused by the separation of the subfloor and floorboards. In this case, try driving screws through the subfloor, into the boards above, to draw the two together. (Make sure the screws reach only about halfway into floorboards.) If this doesn't work, try using concealed nailing from above, or lubricating the squeak area (see below).

Special advice: Before driving nails through hardwood flooring, drill pilot holes that are slightly smaller than the nail size to avoid splitting. Start the pilot hole at the edge of the board and angle it down and toward the center of the board. When refastening stair treads to risers from the top side, drive flooring nails at an angle toward each other. In either case, you can use a nailset to avoid marring board surfaces, and wood putty to cover the nail holes.

Helpful hint: In some cases you may be able to stop the squeak by using powdered graphite, available at hardware or auto parts stores. Spray the graphite into visible cracks in the area of the squeak. This

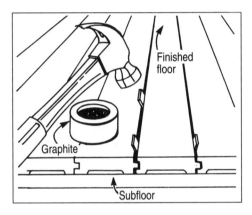

may lubricate the parts that are rubbing together and stop the noise. Another option is to reinforce the tread/riser joints with wooden blocks, using construction adhesive and wood screws.

● ● ●

91 Wood Floor Is Stained

Background: Most stains can be prevented or minimized by keeping wood floors well waxed, and by wiping up any spilled liquid immediately. When removing a stain, always begin at the outer edge and work toward the middle to prevent it from spreading.

What to do: To clean dried milk or food stains, rub the spot with a damp cloth, dry it, and re-wax the floor. For stains caused by standing water, rub with No. 00 steel wool and re-wax. If this fails, sand the spot lightly with fine sandpaper. Clean the spot and surrounding areas using No. 1 steel wool and mineral spirits or a commercial floor cleaner. Let the floor dry, then apply matching finish on floor, feathering it out into surrounding areas. Wax after finish dries. For dark spots, including ink stains and fresh animal stains 1) clean the spot and surrounding area with No. 1 steel wool and mineral spirits or a good floor cleaner; 2) thoroughly wash the stained area with household vinegar, allowing it to soak for 3 or 4 minutes; 3) if the spot remains, sand with fine sandpaper, feather out 3 inches to 4 inches into the surrounding area, re-wax, and polish.

Special advice: If repeated applications of vinegar don't remove a dark spot, apply an oxalic acid solution of 1 ounce acid to 1 quart water directly on the spot. (This is a poisonous solution; use rubber gloves.) Allow solution to stand 1 hour and then sponge the spot with clear water. A second treatment may be needed. If that fails, sand the area and apply a matching finish, feathering it out into the surrounding floor area. Let the finish dry and buff lightly with No. 00 steel wool. Apply a second coat of finish, let it dry, and wax. If the spot still remains, the only option may be to replace the affected flooring. (**Note:** Oxalic acid is a bleaching agent and, if used, the treated floor area will probably need to be restained and refinished to match original color.)

Helpful hint: For heel or caster marks, rub vigorously with fine steel wool and a good floor cleaner, wipe dry, and polish. For shallow cigarette burns, use steel wool moistened with soap and water. For alcohol spots, rub with liquid or paste wax, silver polish, boiled linseed oil, or a cloth barely dampened in ammonia, and then re-wax. For oil or grease stains, rub on a soap with a high lye content, or saturate a piece of cotton with hydrogen peroxide and place it over the stain. Then saturate a second layer of cotton with ammonia and place over the first. Repeat until stain is removed. For chewing gum, crayon, or candle wax, try applying ice until the material is brittle enough to scrape off.

• • •

92 Vinyl Floor Is Stained

Problem: Spill on the floor has resulted in stain, or has potential to stain.

Background: The most effective way to eliminate stains on reinforced vinyl or solid vinyl floor tile is to blot or wipe up spills as soon as possible after they occur. Most spills can be removed with a clean cloth or paper towel dampened with a commercial cleaner or detergent, especially if the floor has a protective coating. However, if certain substances are overlooked or remain on floor for an extended time, the specific procedures listed below may remove or help minimize the stain.

What to do: For tar, asphalt, grease, oil, wax, chewing gum, or crayon stains, use procedures **A, B, F, G.** For ink, lipstick, mustard, catsup, iodine, Mercurochrome, Merthiolate, or alcoholic beverages, use **A, B, C, G.** For oil-based paint, varnish, or shoe polish, use **A, B, D, G.** For nail polish, lacquer or airplane glue, use **A, B, E, G.** For lye, drain cleaners, or detergent concentrates, use **A, B, G.** For rust, use **B, G.**

Procedure A: Blot stain with a clean white absorbent cloth or paper towel, then remove dry or hardened substance with a stiff putty knife or plastic spatula.

Procedure B: Wash the stain with an absorbent cloth or sponge dampened with undiluted commercial cleaner. For heavy residue, scrub with a synthetic scrub pad (like those used for nonstick pans) wetted with cleaner.

Procedure C: Rub the stain with a cloth wetted with rubbing alcohol, rotating the cloth. Don't walk on the area for 30 minutes. If the stain persists, repeat using liquid chlorine laundry bleach.

Procedure D: Rub the stain with a cloth wetted with turpentine. Don't walk on the area for 30 minutes.

Procedure E: Same as Procedure D, except wet the cloth with nail polish remover.

Procedure F: Same as Procedure D, except wet a cloth with lighter fluid.

Procedure G: Rinse the treated area with water, allow it to dry, and apply the floor finish you use regularly.

Special advice: Use these procedures in the order they are given for each type of stain. They may be repeated if you experience difficulty in removing a stain. *Be cautious when working with alcohol, turpentine, lighter fluid, or nail polish remover.* These solvents are highly flammable; do not smoke or use them in the vicinity of an open flame, and provide adequate ventilation for your work area.

Helpful hint: For floors damaged by scrapes or indentations, see entry 93. A permanently stained or damaged tile may be removed and replaced with a spare tile. If 1 or 2 tiles need replacement and spares aren't available, consider exchanging a damaged tile with one located in a closet or beneath an appliance or piece of furniture.

• • •

93 Resilient Floor Is Damaged

Problem: Excessive pressure has resulted in floor damage.

Background: Resilient floors can be permanently marred from indentations or scrapes caused by excessive loads or the movement of equipment, appliances, and furniture that have small or sharp weight-bearing surfaces.

What to do: Remove and replace any existing metal or plastic domes (small weight-bearing surfaces) from the bottom of furniture legs or equipment. Use composition furniture cups under the legs of any heavy furniture, which is more or less permanently located, to keep them from cutting the floor. Casters with rubber wheels are best for frequently moved furniture. A desk chair, for example, should have casters that are 2 inches in diameter with soft rubber treads that are at least ¾ inch wide with easy-swiveling ball bearing action. Equip light furniture with 1¼ inch to 1½ inch-diameter glides that have a smooth, flat base with rounded edges and a flexible pin to maintain flat contact with the floor. For light furniture with slanted legs, attach flat glides with flexible shanks, with the glides parallel to the floor rather than on the slanted leg ends.

Special advice: To replace a damaged floor tile, see entry 91. Roll flooring may be patched satisfactorily with special punches used by professional installers. Generally, the maximum load per square inch of bearing surface is about 40 pounds for asphalt tile, about 75 pounds for reinforced vinyl, and about 250 pounds for solid vinyl tile. For very heavy items that must be moved frequently, check with caster dealers or manufacturers for advice.

Helpful hint: To avoid marring or damaging floor surfaces when moving heavy equipment, furniture, or appliances, place panels of plywood or hardboard over the floor and roll the item over the panels, moving the panels as necessary.

• • •

94 Carpet Is Stained

Problem: Accidental spills have resulted in spots and stain on carpet.

Background: A wide variety of substances can cause spots on carpeting and the procedures used to remove them vary. However, the cleaning procedure for all except ballpoint pen and tar spots begins with removing the excess material. To absorb excess liquid, use a clean white cloth or tissue; for solids, scrape lightly; for powders, vacuum and do not moisten.

What to do: Remove excess as mentioned above, and perform the steps listed in order. In some cases, such as removing inks, a step may be called for a second time if the stain hasn't come out with the first couple of steps. For acids, use procedures **A, C, W, T.** For alcoholic beverages, beer, bleach, syrup or wine, use **C, V, T.** For ammonia or alkali, use **V, C, W, T.** For animal urine, use **W, V, C, W, T.** For ballpoint pen begin with **X** and then use **D.** For grease, use **D.** For tar, begin with **D.** For blood, use **W, C, A, V, T.** For butter or margarine, use **D, C, W, T.** For candy, use **C, V, W, T.** For catsup, cough syrup, or wet water-based paint, use **C, W, T.** For chewing gum, use **G, D.** For chocolate, use **C, V, Z, D.** For cocktails, use **C, W, T, Z, D.** For coffee, use **C, V, T, D.**

For cosmetics and oils, use procedures **D, C, A, V, T.** For dye (water), use **C, A, V, T, P.** For egg, glue (water), or soft drinks, use **C, A, V, T.** For fruit or fruit juices, use **C, A, V, W, T.** For furniture polish, use **X, D, C, A, V, T.** For gravy, use **C, Z, D.** For household cement (solvent), use **X, D.** For ice cream or vomit, use **C, A, V, T, Z, D.** For inks (water), use **C, W, T, Z, P.** For inks (solvent) or nail polish, use **D, X, D, P.** For lipstick, use **D, C, A, V, T, P.** For milk, use **C,**

A, V, W, T, D. For Merthiolate, use **X, D, C, T.** For mustard, use **C, V, T, Z, D.** For wet oil-based paint, use **D.** For dried paint, use **X, D, C.** For perfume, use **D, C, V, T.** For sauces or salad dressing, use **D, C, V, T, Z, D.** For shoe polish, use **X, D, C, A, V, T.** For tea, use **C, V, T, D.** For unknown stains, use **C, Z, D, P.**

Procedure A: Apply ammonia solution (1 tablespoon household ammonia to 1 cup water) and blot.

Procedure C: Use carpet shampoo solution diluted according to label directions.

Procedure D: Use dry-cleaning fluid.

Procedure G: Freeze residue with aerosol chewing gum remover, dry ice (handled carefully with gloves on), or with ice cubes in a plastic bag. Shatter with a blunt object, and vacuum up chips immediately while they are still hard.

Procedure P: Call professional rug cleaner for advice.

Procedure T: Place ½-inch layer of white absorbent material or tissues over damp area under a weight for several hours.

Procedure V: White vinegar solution (1 tablespoon to 1 cup lukewarm water) and blot.

Procedure W: Rinse with plain water and blot.

Procedure X: Use paint, oil, or grease remover.

Procedure Z: Allow carpet to dry.

Special advice: Cigarette burns generally must be repaired by replacing the charred area (professional installers have special punches to do this). If the burn is superficial, you may improve the appearance by brushing the surface and carefully snipping charred tufts with shears.

Helpful hint: Don't use common household detergents, such as soap, ammonia, washing soda, or strong household cleaners on carpets. They may damage the carpet fiber, and many will leave a sticky film that will cause rapid resoiling to occur.

●●●

95 Upholstery Is Stained

Problem: Spills have resulted in stains in upholstered furniture.

Background: Upholstery requires maintenance to stay attractive, including regular vacuuming before soil works its way into fibers. Remove spots immediately because the longer they remain, the harder they are to get out. Cleanability labels, when found, may designate **W** (use water-based cleaner), **S** (use solvent cleaner), **W-S** (use water-based or solvent cleaner), or **X** (vacuum only). With **W,** spot-clean using only the foam of a water-based cleaning agent, such as a mild detergent or commercial nonsolvent upholstery shampoo. Use sparingly and avoid over-wetting. Apply foam with a soft brush in a circular motion and vacuum when dry. With **S,** spot-clean with a mild water-free solvent or dry-cleaning product. Use sparingly in a well-ventilated room.

What to do: The following general guidelines use the symbol **D** for a detergent and water solution of ½ teaspoon liquid hand dishwashing detergent per quart of warm water (water-based commercial shampoos, either liquid or foam, can also be used); **S** for non-flammable liquid dry-cleaning solvent; **V** for 1 part white vinegar to 1 part water; **A** for 1 tablespoon non-sudsing household ammonia to 1 cup of water; **AL** for rubbing alcohol, and **W** for water. Caution: *Follow label directions with dry-cleaning solvents and household ammonia. Alcohol can affect some dyes.*

To remove stains, use the cleaning agents following the type of stain listed below, in order. Start with the first and continue working with it as long as the stain is being removed. If the agent being used is effective, stop there. If not, try the second agent given and so on. Pretest cleaning agents and, if in doubt, seek the advice of a professional upholstery cleaner.

Acids: **W, A, W.**

Alcoholic Beverages: **D, W, AL, W.**

Ammonia: **W, V, W.**

Blood: **D, A, V, W.**

Catsup: **S, D, A, W.**

Chocolate: **S, D, A, V, W.**

Coffee and tea: **D, V, W, AL, W.**

Cologne or perfume: **W, D, W, AL, W.**

Cosmetics: **S, D, A, V, W, AL, W.**

Crayon: **S, D.**

Dyes or food coloring: **D, A, V, W, AL, W.**

Fruit or fruit juices: **D, V, W, AL, W.**

Furniture polish or stain: **S, D, A, V, W.**

Glue (casein/white): **D, V, W, AL.**

Ice cream: **S, W, D, A, W.**

Ink (India or felt tip): **S, D, A, V, W.**

Ink (writing): **D, V, W, AL, W, A, W.**

Lipstick: **S, D, A, V, W, AL, W.**

Meat juice or gravy: **S, D, A, W.**

Milk with cream: **S, D, A, W.**

Mustard: **S, W, D, V, W.**

Ointment: **S, W, D, A, W.**

Oils (butter, fats): **S, D, A, W.**

Paint (oil-based): **S, D, A, W.**

Paint (water-based): **D, A, W.**

Pencil: **S, W, D, A, W.**

Rubber cement: **S.**

Salad dressing: **S, D, A, W.**

Shoe polish: **S, D, V, W.**

Soft drinks: **D, A, V, W, AL, W.**

Soot: **S, D, A.**

Tar: **S, W, D, A, W.**

Urine: **D, A, W, AL, W.**

Vomit: **D, A, W.**

Wine or liquor: **D, V, W, AL, W.**

Special advice: For candle wax, chill with a plastic bag of ice, scrape off as much as possible, and sponge with a dry-cleaning solvent until all the wax is removed. An alternate method is to cover the wax with paper towels and iron at low temperatures, replacing paper towels and continuing until no wax melts; then sponge with dry-cleaning solvent. For chewing gum, chill with ice for easier removal; then blot with dry-cleaning solvent. For fingernail polish, use amyl acetate (banana oil) available from drugstores; ask for the chemically pure type. (A non-oil fingernail polish remover is safe for most fabrics unless it contains acetone, which will dissolve acetate fabrics and swell modacrylics.) Dry-cleaning solvents will also remove some types of polish.

Helpful hint: When the stain is all gone, be sure chemicals are thoroughly removed. If water rings occur, moisten the entire stained area with a white vinegar and water solution. Let stand a few minutes, then sponge with water. Dry the spots thoroughly.

● ● ●

96 Special Coverings Stained

Problem: Spills have occurred on coverings such as velvet, leather, or vinyl.

Background: Dirt and spills on special furniture coverings need to be handled with caution. Velvet, a fabric construction technique, can present problems with at-home methods. In general, there are 2 types of leather: leather that has a surface coating, and leather that has very little surface protection. The way you handle spills on leather will depend on which type you have. Vinyl coverings also require special care when cleaning or removing stains.

What to do: Velvets with stain-resistant finishes usually can be spot-cleaned with a cloth dampened with water. With rayon velvets, avoid water; they can sometimes be spot-cleaned with dry-cleaning solvents. Note that stain-removal products often warn against their use on velvets, so test for discoloration or pile distortion in a hidden area before applying one to a stain. Some adhesives used to make flocked velvet are affected by dry-cleaning solvents, and many velvets can't be cleaned with water-based cleaning agents. Dry powder cleaners may be used but, because of possible damage, read labels, pretest all cleaners, and consult a professional cleaner if in doubt.

To clean treated or surface-coated leather, dust with a dry cloth regularly or occasionally clean with a solution of mild soap and warm water. Wipe suds away thoroughly with a clean, damp cloth; then lightly buff with a dry cloth. Most stains can be wiped away with a damp sponge. (Avoid using leather creams, saddle soaps, or oil treatments on treated leather unless the manufacturer states otherwise.) With untreated leathers, or those with limited surface protection, an art-gum eraser may remove ordinary dirt. An uncoated surface will absorb liquids and oils, and stains may be impossible to remove. (Avoid using strong detergents, furniture polishes, or dry-cleaning solvents.)

Vinyls can be cleaned with a clean, damp cloth. For heavier soil, sponge with a warm water and mild detergent solution. (Allow the sudsy mixture to remain for a few minutes, then wipe with a damp cloth and polish with a dry one; don't let the mixture seep into the upholstery padding.) Rinse well, and pay special attention to areas in contact with hair oils and tonics because they may make vinyls brittle. Household cleaners may be effective on very soiled vinyl, but cleaners with ammonia or chlorine may cause damage, and those with abrasives may scratch. Dry-cleaning solvents can cause the fabric to stiffen and its layers to separate. Check labels for products that are marked "safe for all vinyl"; some special auto-uphol-stery cleaners may also be safe to use.

Special advice: Nail polish and polish remover will damage vinyls permanently if left on the surface. Sponge with synthetic turpentine or mineral spirits (test first). Ballpoint pen marks may be permanent, but you can try rubbing them with alcohol. If this doesn't work, cover the area with a clean, white cloth soaked in a 6% solution of hydrogen peroxide for about 30 minutes (also test first). Felt tip markers will usually leave permanent stains, even if wiped up immediately. However, they may respond to treatment with mineral spirits (test first). Some marker inks may be removed with water.

Helpful hint: Vinyls sometimes absorb dyes from colored objects that they come in contact with. Use white cloths for cleaning. And, after using a cleaning agent, wash and rinse the surface with water.

●●●

97 Structural Wood Is Rotting

Problem: Excessive moisture is causing wood in home to deteriorate.

Background: Decaying wood is more permeable to moisture, and therefore, is more subject to further damage and decay. Discoloration on wood may be mold (see entry 98); however, symptoms of wood decay are also often recognized by color. Both white and brown rot are serious and deserve treatment or warrant replacement of the wood.

- White rot, the most difficult damage to recognize, is probably the worst form of wood decay. Wood with white rot appears somewhat whiter than normal, and sometimes has dark lines bordering the light discoloration. Though affected wood doesn't always shrink or collapse, in advanced stages, some cracking occurs across the grain.
- Brown rot appears as a brown color or brown streaks on the face of the wood or end grains. In advanced stages, the wood looks very damaged, with the surface shrinking and collapsing and with cracks across the grain.
- Soft rot and blue stain are less damaging, slower-acting forms of wood decay that tend to be more active on the surface. With soft rot, the wood surface appears soft and profusely cracked, resembling driftwood in color. A blue stain indicates somewhat weakened wood, with blue, brownish black, or steel gray staining. The discoloration is not a surface stain; it penetrates the wood cells.

What to do: The most common method of detecting external decay is the pick test, using a sharp, pointed metal tool. An icepick, small chisel, or small screwdriver can be jabbed into wood and used to pry or lift wood slivers. A splintering break of wetted wood indicates soundness, while a sharp break across the wood grain suggests decay. Decayed wood breaks out with less resistance, is easily penetrated by a pick, and may have a rough or fibrous surface. When cut with a saw, wood affected with even early stages of decay produces a rougher finish cut than wood that is not infected. When jabbing wood with a pick, start at ground level or below and work up. Check whether areas that look soft have other symptoms of decay, such as color and texture changes.

Special advice: Another test is to tap the wood's surface; good, dry wood produces a sharp, clear, almost ringing sound and wet or decaying wood produces a dull, dead, soft sound.

Helpful hint: If you detect wood rot caused by excess moisture, try to correct the source of the problem, whether it is moisture from inside the house or moisture leakage into the house. You also may need to take steps to reduce humidity movement by stopping air leakage into wall, ceiling, and window cavities and by reducing high humidity with ventilation and membrane vapor retarders installed in crawl spaces, below ground walls, and basement areas.

●●●

98 Mold and Mildew Inside Home

Problem: High humidity levels result in mildew growth, which causes damage and potential allergic reaction.

Background: Mold growths that develop under favorable conditions are often seen as a discoloration, ranging in color from white to orange, and from green to brown to black. If mold can't be seen, it may be recognized as a musty odor. Mold growth can cause soiling and deterioration of appliances and other items in a home. The buildup of mold in air cooling and humidifying units, plumbing fixtures, condensation trays, and drains can cause serious and often costly mechanical problems. Mold can discolor paint, weaken fabrics, and degrade foodstuffs. It can also lead to odor problems.

What to do: Relative humidity levels above 70% are optimal for indoor mold buildup. Controlling the problem in a home usually involves three steps 1) eliminating moisture from inside and outside sources; 2) removing mold colonies and spores, and 3) installing a mechanical ventilation system. One method of determining whether your home has a potential problem is to measure the relative humidity inside your house.

Optimal levels are 15% if outside temperature is -20°F, 20% if -10°F, 25% if +0°F, 30% if +10°F, and 35% to 40% if +20°F. Also visually inspect for mold colonies, including areas of stagnant water, and room corners.

Regularly clean appliances that have water pans or use moisture. Other steps to reduce humidity include turning humidifiers down or off, using range and bath exhaust fans while cooking or bathing, cooking with covered pans, installing a fresh-air intake duct to bring in drier outside air, venting dryers to the outside, sealing cracks in house or vapor retarders, and not using unvented kerosene or gas heaters.

Special advice: To remove existing mold, clean affected areas with a homemade solution of ⅔ cup cleanser (such as Ajax or Comet), ⅓ cup nonphosphate detergent, 1 quart 5% sodium hypochlorite (such as Clorox or Hilex), and 3 quarts warm water. Brush solution onto affected area with a medium-sized soft brush. After cleaning, rinse thoroughly with fresh water and, if possible, paint area with a mold-resistant paint.

Helpful hint: If a member of your household is allergic to mold, adding an air cleaner can help remove mold spores present. (Heating ducts need to be cleaned before adding an air cleaner.) If carpet, upholstery, ceiling tiles, or other porous furnishings are contaminated, it is best to discard them rather than attempting disinfection because mold spores are likely to remain.

• • •

99 Wood Screws Won't Tighten

Problem: Screws in hinges, furniture, or moveable fittings work loose and won't stay tightened.

Background: Wood screws come in a wide variety of sizes and head types, including flat head, round head, and oval head, and may be slotted or Phillips type. They are threaded about two-thirds of their length. The Phillips heads work better with a drill or power screwdriver unit. Common screws will range in diameter thickness from No. 2 (small) to No. 16 (large), and in length from about ¼ inch to 2¼ inches. Generally screws are sized so that two-thirds will go into the base material, or second member, to which the surface piece is being fastened. It is a simple matter to tighten loose screws, but if the threads do not hold, extra work is necessary.

What to do: If the threads are worn out, or the screw has become loose in its original hole, try using a larger

screw. In some cases this may not be possible, because the holes in the metal fittings or the thickness of the wood will not allow it. The options are to fill the screw hole with a wood plug, plastic wood, or steel wool. Even toothpicks or wooden safety matches with the heads broken off can work. Fill the hole with glue before inserting tapered wood plugs, toothpicks, or match stems. Once the glue has set, trim the wood material off flush with wood. Predrill a hole slightly smaller than the screw size when either wood plugs or plastic wood are to be used. With steel wool, insert a small amount into the screw hole and then reinsert the screw.

Special advice: Paraffin or wax can be used to lubricate screws for easier turning. (Do not use soap because it can cause the screw to rust.) Also don't hammer in screws part way; it's best to use a starter hole or, even better, to use a drilled pilot and shank holes. Many woodworking books have charts showing the drill bit sizes to use for pilot and clearance holes.

Helpful hint: You can buy special drill bits at home centers and hardware stores which drill the pilot hole, clearance hole, and countersink all in one operation. These are helpful if you need to drill many holes.

HOME EXTERIORS

●●●●●●●●●●●●●●

100 Roof Shingles Leak

Problem: Home's roof leaks.

Background: Damaged or missing asphalt or fiberglass shingles can cause roof leaks. Seriously consider the risks of doing the job yourself, especially if the roof is steep, if the repairs seem complicated, or if you do not have the equipment you need (such as the right ladders). Try to repair asphalt shingles when the weather is relatively warm, because they can become brittle in cold weather.

What to do: If the roof is leaking, determine the general area by looking inside the attic. Shingles with only small cracks may be fixed with roofing cement. If a shingle is damaged or torn, but does not need replacing, raise it and apply a good amount of roofing cement to the underside. Press the shingle into place and nail it down with galvanized roofing nails. If the shingle needs replacing, raise the shingles above the damaged one. Pull the nails from the damaged shingle with a claw hammer. (If the nails can't be reached

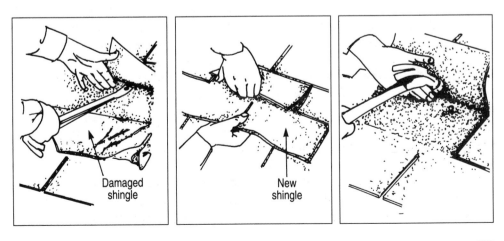

Damaged shingle

New shingle

with a hammer, cut off with a hack-saw blade or use a flat pry bar to remove them.) Remove the shingle, install the new shingle, and nail in place.

Special advice: Generally use 2 nails to secure each tab of a shingle strip; this means you would use 6 nails for each full strip. The shingle should be blind nailed, or covered by the upper shingles when they are lowered in place. After nailing, remember to apply a dab of asphalt cement over the nailheads, before lowering the upper shingles into place.

Helpful hint: Sometimes, if you don't have a replacement shingle, you can use a section of metal flashing under the damaged shingle. Slip it underneath and nail it to the roof, then coat the underside of the damaged shingle with roofing cement and press it into place.

• • •

101 Wood Shingles Damaged

Problem: Roof leaks because wooden shingles are damaged or missing.

Background: If the roof leaks, locate the trouble spot from the inside. If the wood shingle is cracked, it may be better to repair the crack than to try to replace the shingle. Larger

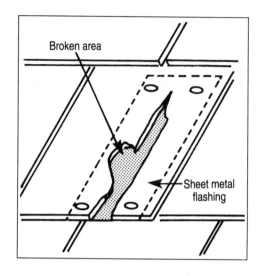

Broken area

Sheet metal flashing

cracks may be repaired with a sheet metal patch underneath. If damaged shingles are beyond repair, they must be replaced. This can be more tricky than repairing a cracked shingle.

What to do: If the crack is ¼ inch or less, pull out loose splinters so only large, solid pieces remain. Check the roof under the shingles to determine where the nails should go. Then butt the solid pieces together tightly and nail the split shingle together with galvanized roofing nails. Don't drive the nail heads into the shingle or damage its surface. For wide cracks, you can drive a square piece of sheet metal or roofing paper up under the shingle so that the upper part goes beyond the upper edge of the crack, then proceed as you would to repair a small crack.

Special advice: To replace a shingle, use a screwdriver or chisel to break up the old shingle. Remove the pieces and use a hacksaw blade to cut nails off flush with the wood slats or sheathing. (You may have to pry up the shingle above enough to get at all the nails.) Cut a replacement shingle and, using a wood block and hammer, drive it into position. Nail it in place and apply a dab of asphalt cement to cover the nailheads.

Helpful hint: Also check over the roof for loose shingles. Nail these down securely. You can avoid cracking shingles when nailing by predrilling holes where the nails will be placed.

● ● ●

102 Ice Dams Form on Roof

Problem: Ice dams form at roof edges, causing backup of snow water which can damage home.

Background: Ice dams cause millions of dollars of damage to homes in northern areas every year. They are especially prevalent when snow and weather conditions react with poor attic ventilation and insulation. Snow melts next to the shingles, runs down under the top layer of snow, and freezes near the edge of the roof. Additional snow water backs up under the shingles, resulting in soaked insulation; stained, cracked, or spalled plaster or wallboard; damp, smelly, and rotting wall cavities; and stained, blistered, or peeling wall paint inside and outside the house.

What to do: The most effective remedy is to improve both attic ventilation and insulation to keep roof temperatures as close to the outside temperature as possible. All other emergency measures are short-term, and have drawbacks. They may include using a roof rake, hosing ice dams with tap water on a warm day, or having the roof steamed. Removing snow from roofs can be dangerous, water runoff from hosing can damage shrubbery, and steam can expand and contract the roof deck.

Room ceilings should be insulated heavily to minimize heat losses and reduce attic temperatures, and the attic area should be ventilated sufficiently so outside air sweeps out any warmed attic air. Make sure insulation doesn't lose effectiveness because of bridging, wires, or ceiling fixtures. Also check for uninsulated chimneys, gas vents, warm exhaust piping, or other sources of heat. (A rule of thumb is that attics should have 1 square inch of ventilation opening for each square foot of ceiling area.)

Special advice: Heating cables, arranged in a sawtooth pattern near the eaves, are sometimes installed to help prevent ice dams. They are generally ineffective: melting is limited to only a few inches from the cable, melting often causes secondary ice dams higher on the roof, and cables use large amounts of energy. *Never chop through the ice dams down to the shingles, or use a blowtorch, because you may cause roof damage.*

Helpful hint: Just improving attic insulation will not prevent ice dams; it must be done in conjunction with adequate ventilation using ridge vents, soffit vents, roof louvers, or power vents. Insulation also must not block air passages, especially immediately above outside walls.

• • •

103 Door Won't Close Correctly

Problem: Door in home binds, sticks, or won't latch properly.

Background: If the door frame has become distorted, your door may stick at the corners or be hard to close, and its latches may not fit the strikeplate. A door that binds or sticks against a door frame can also be caused by loose or ineffective hinges, by the frame settling, by the door or frame swelling, or by the door warping. Hinges that are loose, either on the top or bottom, will allow a door to sag. If a door is too tight on the hinge edge, it will bind against the hinge jamb. A door that has warped inward or outward at the hinge edge will be hard to close. If a door frame spreads because the home has settled, it may widen the doorway so the bolt in the lock may not reach the strikeplate. If partitions next to, or below, a door frame settle or shrink, the frame can move slightly and move the strikeplate with it while the door and lock stay in position.

What to do: Check for loose hinges, by pulling and pushing the opened door away from and toward the hinges. If the hinges move, you can either tighten the original screws, insert wood plugs in the screw holes, or substitute longer screws. Also check for a loose strikeplate or lock faceplate screws. If the door still binds after tightening the screws, you may be able to sand or plane down the high spot (or call a finish carpenter if you don't trust your skills). Mark where it binds, remove the door and check to see where the door finish has been rubbed. Sand or, if necessary, plane lightly from the edges toward the center, then replace the door to check for fit. (Remove as little as needed because wood will shrink as humidity drops.) When the door works properly, refinish as appropriate.

Special advice: If a door binds at the hinge edge, and has clearance on the lock side, you can try inserting cardboard shims under the outer hinge leaves (those set in the jamb). If the lock bolt does not enter the hole in the strikeplate, check to see if it strikes the plate too high or too low. Take out the screws, remove the strikeplate, and file the metal opening until it is large enough to accommodate the bolt. If more than ¼ inch needs to be removed, it may be better to reset the strikeplate. (Also see entry 104 about locks and keys.)

Helpful hint: If the margin of a door is even along the top and bottom edges, and the hinges are firm, either the hinge or lock edge can be planed. However, it's usually best to plane the hinge edge, because hinges are easier to remove and reinstall than locks.

•••

104 Key Doesn't Work in Door

Problem: Door won't open because of binding or broken key, a stuck bolt, or a frozen lock.

Background: Like most other mechanical devices, keys and locks can wear out or become damaged. Sometimes lock problems are caused by a misaligned door. To prevent lock problems, periodically inspect them, tighten loose screws, apply lock lubricant, and make adjustments as necessary to strikeplates. Excessively loose tubular or cylinder locksets, or locks that seize the key, may be candidates for replacement; however, sometimes a locksmith can replace worn tumblers and springs.

What to do: If the lock is frozen, try warming the key and reinserting it,

or try squirting alcohol into the keyhole. When a key breaks in a lock, it is often because it was not pushed in completely before turning, or the wrong key was pushed into the lock. If part of the key stays inside the lock, remove the cylinder and try pushing the key part out with a fine pin from the shaft end. When keys bend, it may be caused by a poorly made duplicate key. If an original key works in the lock, have the duplicate remade. Binding can also be caused by worn tumblers. If you think this is the problem, remove the cylinder and take it to a locksmith. If the key turns, but the bolt sticks, check to make sure the bolt isn't blocked by paint. If the bolt can't move because the door is misaligned, check and align the door (see entry 103).

Special advice: To help avoid lock problems, try to make all keys easily identified. When having duplicate keys made, go to a qualified locksmith who uses top-quality blanks. (Having at least 1 extra duplicate key kept in a secure place can prevent an emergency.) When replacing locksets, spend more for the best quality you can afford. Locks can be lubricated with graphite (in a pinch, rub keys with graphite from a wooden pencil) or with fine oil sold for that purpose. Don't use regular lubricating oil.

Helpful hint: When locking up the home, don't lock all other doors from the inside; if the door locked with a key doesn't work you won't be able to gain entry to the inside of the home.

• • •

105 Screens Punctured or Torn

Problem: Accidental contact with screen has resulted in small holes or tears in screening.

Background: Screens with smaller areas of damage that allow insects inside the home can often be easily repaired to avoid the time and expense of replacing the entire screen (see entry 106). A number of repair options are available, depending on the screening material and the size of the damaged area. Ready-made patching kits are available for both metal and plastic-type screening materials. Or use the following procedure to repair a metal screen.

What to do: First trim the damaged area of the metal screen to make the edges smooth. Then cut a rectangular patch of the same type of material, about 1 inch larger than the hole. Next remove 2 or 3 outside wires on the metal screen patch so only single strands exist for about ½ inch on all sides of the patch. Put the patch over the end of a block of wood and bend the single strands 90°, all in one direction, on all sides of the patch. Trim the bent single strands so they are about ¼ inch long and put the patch over the hole

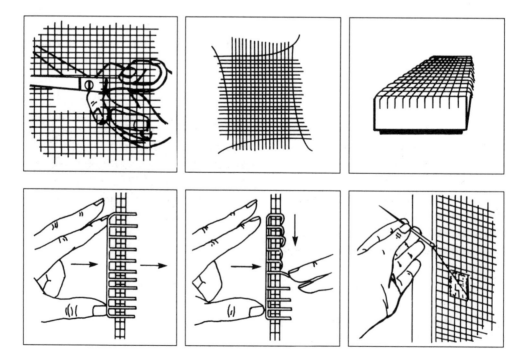

from the outside. Push the bent wires through the screen and, holding the patch tight against the screen, bend down the wire ends toward the center of the hole. (You may need a helper to hold the patch while you bend the wires.)

Special advice: An alternate method, if the damage is a small tear or hole, is to mend by stitching back and forth with a fine wire pulled from extra screening material, or with nylon thread or fine monofilament fishing line.

Helpful hint: When making patches with wire, the result will look better if the wires of the patch are lined up with the wires of the screen. If the wires are only pulled apart, working them back into position with a pencil may solve the problem without patchwork.

• • •

age. Newer screens may suffer damage from abuse and their wood or metal frames may need repair. Note: *Broken-out screens on second or third stories of homes should be fixed promptly, especially if small children are present.* Though screens are not intended to keep children from falling, screens either damaged or not in place may increase chances of injuries due to falls. Newer screening material available include aluminum and fiberglass.

What to do: Most local hardware stores offer screen-repair service. If you do the repair yourself, you may need a splining tool, available at your hardware store. With wood-frame screens, remove the moulding from the exterior side and pull out the old screening. To get the new screen tight, set up 2 sawhorses with two 2×4s between them the width of the frame. Lay 2×4s under the bottom and top ends of the frame, then

106 Screens Need Replacement

Problem: Screen section is loose from frame, has been pushed out, or has suffered damage beyond the scope of small patch repairs.

Background: Older screens may deteriorate from weathering and rust and become vulnerable to dam-

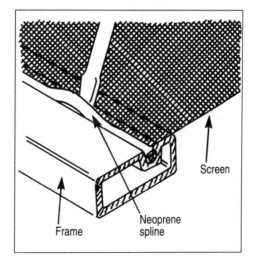

Screen

Frame

Neoprene spline

use C-clamps in the middle of each side to bow the frame. Begin by attaching the top, bottom, and sides and by pushing the screening into the spline, if there is one, and with staples. Trim off any excess screen, release the clamps, and replace the moulding.

With metal-frame screens, screening is held in place by a vinyl spline, which is in a groove along the frame. When buying new screening, also buy new spline material of the same size. Use a screwdriver to remove the old spline and screening. Press the new screening in place with a splining tool, using the convex wheel for an aluminum screen, or the concave wheel for a fiberglass screen.

Special advice: To remove mouldings from wood frames without splitting them, use a small screwdriver, putty knife, or a thin, flat pry bar. Break any paint seals with a utility knife, then work under the moulding near the brads that hold it. Remove the perimeter moulding first because the center moulding may be wedged between the side pieces.

Helpful hint: When replacing the screen, also check the frame for loose or broken corners. Mending plates made of heavy sheet metal for strengthening frames are available in either flat or angle versions.

• • •

107 Manual Garage Door Won't Open

Problem: A manually operated garage door will not open when the latch is turned and you attempt to lift it up.

Background: Garage doors, whether operated manually or with electric openers, are the heaviest moving equipment around the home. They depend on 1 of 2 types of springs to operate. Some mechanisms use extension springs that stretch like rubber bands to slow the closing of the door, and then contract to help lift the weight of the door when it is opened. Other doors use torsion springs that wind up like the springs in window shades to handle the weight of the door. Caution: *If springs break, be careful when closing the door; the door's weight will cause it to fall quickly and heavily.*

A garage door may stick for many reasons, ranging from the key not working properly in the lock or a faulty latch mechanism, to more serious problems such as broken cables, bent or loose tracks, and jammed rollers.

What to do: If the outside handle won't turn, it may be because the key or the latch are worn out (see entry 104). If the handle turns, but the door won't lift, enter through the service door if there is one, and check the mechanism on the inside of the door. The problem may be a track bent inward which will not allow the horizontal bar (turned by the outside handle) to clear its slot. The solution, in this case, is to carefully bend the track back with a tool such as a pipe wrench. If that doesn't work, or if the problem is more serious, it is best to call a garage door technician.

If the door opens, but takes more than a little effort to lift, the springs may need adjustment. *However, attempting to adjust garage door springs can be dangerous and should be done by a professional.* Adjustments on torsion springs can be especially dangerous because special tools are required to do the job. The brackets that hold springs to the garage frame are also under tension; attempting to make adjustments to these brackets also can be hazardous.

Special advice: Do not attempt to solve difficult door-lifting problems by simply installing an electric opener. Call a technician to balance the door, even if you plan to install an opener. (Openers required to lift heavy, unbalanced weights may develop mechanical problems.) Regular, light maintenance can extend your garage door's life. Check the cables for shiny spots, and be sure that strands at connections are not partially broken. Pulley wheels for cables should roll, not skid.

Also check the tracks to see that they are not bent or loose where they attach to the garage, and that the wheels roll freely. See that all bolts and screws are tight, and that all cotter pins are in place. Lubricate pulley bearings, wheel bearings, and door hinges with lightweight household oil or a spray silicone.

Helpful hint: To check the balance of a garage door, start with door closed. (If your door is operated by electronic opener, disconnect its release mechanism so you can open it by hand.) Lift the door halfway up. It should lift smoothly, with little resistance, and it should stay open when it is 3 to 4 feet above the floor. If it doesn't, it is out of balance and should be adjusted by a professional.

• • •

108 Garage Door Opener Quits

Problem: The automatic opener does not open the garage door.

Background: An electronic garage door opener may not activate because its power supply is interrupted, its antenna is out of position, its transmitter is defective, its remote battery is expired, or its push-button switch inside the garage is defective. First make sure the unit's receptacle inside the garage is receiving power, and that the opener is plugged in.

What to do: To determine if the transmitter or its battery is bad, simply see if the opener operates when the push button inside the garage is activated. If it works with the push button, next check to see that the unit's antenna is not bent out of position. Try replacing the transmitter's battery. If the transmitter still doesn't work, its button may be defective. Try cleaning it with electrical contact cleaner. If that doesn't correct the problem, you will most likely need to replace it. Conversely, if the transmitter works but the push button inside the garage doesn't, turn off the power and clean the push button with electrical contact cleaner. If that doesn't fix it, turn off all power and replace the switch simply by removing and detaching the 2 wires that are under the screws on the back, and reinstalling a new switch.

Special advice: When a power failure traps your car inside the garage, pull the emergency release mechanism located on the opener track. Usually, this will be a cord hanging down between the opener motor and the door. Pull the disconnect cord down and away from the door to release it. Important: *If you disengage the emergency release during a power failure, be sure to also unplug the garage door opener.* After the power is back on, pull on the emergency release again to re-engage the opener. Make sure all drivers in your household know how to use the emergency release mechanism.

Helpful hint: For routine adjustments, see entry 109 and consult the opener owner's manual. If you don't

have an owner's manual, contact the manufacturer and request a copy for your specific model. The opener model number should be on the back of the power unit.

●●●

109 Garage Door Opener Won't Close

Problem: Garage door opener automatically reverses as soon as it closes, with no obstruction in its path.

Background: All garage door openers must have a reversing mechanism. If your opener doesn't have one, replace it. If the opener reverses and refuses to keep the door closed, the "sensitivity," "open," or "close" knobs may be out of adjustment. *Important: This safety feature should be tested regularly so the opener closes the door, but does not exert dangerous force which could lead to serious injury or death.*

What to do: First set the "close" knob so the door makes full contact with the floor. To test the sensitivity adjustment, open the door and place a 1-inch thick piece of wood flat on the floor in the door's path at about the center of the door. If you don't have a piece of wood 1-inch thick, use a 2×4. The door should reverse and open the door when it strikes the wood. To test the force of the opener, repeat the test with a corrugated carton under the center of the door. The opener should reverse the door when it contacts the carton without crushing it. If, after experimenting with adjustments, the opener doesn't reverse readily, have it repaired or replaced.

Special advice: The sensitivity knob should be adjusted, beginning at the minimum pressure setting, so that the door will close without reversing. The door should reverse within 2 seconds after hitting an obstruction. Should the sensitivity need to be raised to maximum pressure setting, do not use the opener and have the system checked by a technician for problems such as worn tracks or broken springs. (See entries 107 and 108 for maintenance suggestions.)

Helpful hint: Discuss garage-door safety with children. Explain the danger of being trapped under the door, and do not let them play with or use the transmitter or push-button switch. Teach them never to play under or near an open garage door. The push button should be at least 5 feet from the floor so it is out of children's reach. Always keep the door in sight until it completely closes.

HOME PEST CONTROL

●●●●●●●●●●●●●●

110 Termites Inside Home

Problem: Wood materials in home structure are threatened by termites.

Background: Termites are the most destructive insects to wood in buildings. There are drywood termites, which can live without moisture, and the subterranean, or ground-nesting, termites which are a serious problem in southern states. Subterranean termites live in colonies in the ground and need moisture to survive. They may build earthen tunnels from the ground up to the wood, and they will sometimes completely eat away the inside of a piece of wood while leaving the outside surface intact. Chemicals for protecting against and controlling termites are toxic and should be applied with extreme caution, preferably by an experienced technician.

What to do: Check for termites at least twice a year. Call an exterminator to identify any large numbers of flying insects that you can't identify during spring and summer (termite mating season). Look for earthen tunnelings along masonry foundation and basement walls, around openings where pipes enter walls, and along the surfaces of metal pipes. Check all cracks in slabs and loose mortar in masonry walls. Also check all joints where wood meets with concrete or masonry at walls, slabs, or piers.

Inspect all wood and wood structures that are near the ground, especially those that touch the house, such as fences, wood trellises, and carports. Examine crawl spaces that provide moist conditions, as well as windowsills, door thresholds, porches, and the underside of stairs. (Be on the lookout for peeling and blistering paint.) If you suspect that wood has termite damage, probe with an icepick or penknife. If the point penetrates to a depth of ½ inch with only hand pressure, it's a good indication of wood damage from termites.

Special advice: When chemical treatments are necessary, the procedure is to dig a trench about 1-foot wide and 3-feet deep next to the foundation wall and pour insecticide against the exposed wall surface and into the trench as it backfills. (Check with an exterminator or your local county extension office for recommended chemicals.) The chemical solution is also applied at locations where wood and masonry meet at a joint, and to areas that have earthen floors. Note: *If chemicals are used inside the home, the room or space must be well ventilated and vacated for a period of time.*

To help prevent termites from becoming established, direct all surface water away from the home, allowing no water to accumulate at the foundation. Cover the earth of unpaved basements with plastic film, 4 mil or heavier. Crawl spaces should be at least 2 feet high and kept well ventilated. Keep untreated wood no closer than 6 inches to the ground. Seal all openings where pipes pass through foundations or walls of the house with caulking compound. Seal any cracks or points of loose mortar in masonry walls. If there is a termite shield around the foundation it should be straightened and turned down at least 2 inches at about a 45° angle.

Helpful hint: To help reduce termite problems, make sure all scraps of lumber or stumps are removed when a building project is completed. Also keep crawl spaces clear of wood scraps.

●●●

111 Fleas Inside Home

Problem: Fleas in home are infesting pets or biting people.

Background: Fleas are tiny brown wingless insects, about the size of a common pinhead. They can jump more than a foot horizontally and their hard bodies are almost impossible to crush. All adult fleas are parasitic and must feed on the blood of an animal, such as a dog or cat, to live and reproduce. Small populations may not be noticed, but when numbers increase they may leave the animal and bite humans. Annoying flea infestations may also occur 1 to 3 weeks after a pet has been removed from the home (fleas turn to humans as a food source), after a pet and owner have been away, when an infested pet develops a high temperature (fleas leave the animal), or when fleas from a neighbor's pet collect on your animal.

What to do: People have differing reactions to flea bites; women and preteen children seem most affected. Flea bites, which are rarely felt, will occur in clusters, particularly where clothing fits tightly on the body. Hard, red, itchy spots may surround the bite and persist for about a week. To locate where adult fleas are, walk through suspected areas wearing white socks. The dark-colored fleas will show up against the socks as they jump from the floor.

Eradication includes sanitation and control using insecticides. Persistent infestations, however, are best handled by a pest-control specialist. Clean pet living areas regularly and thoroughly, removing manure, debris, lint, and hair. Destroy old bedding material and keep pets clean and well groomed. Thoroughly vacuum infested areas and along baseboards, carpet edges, around heat registers, and under and within furniture. Destroy vacuum-bag contents and apply an approved insecticide. Insecticides are available for use indoors, outside, and on pets. (Check with your local extension service for recommendations.) Treat both cats and dogs at the same time, and concentrate applications at the base of the tail between the rear legs. If the infestation is heavy, remove rugs, overstuffed furniture and mattresses from rooms, and air them outdoors in a dry, sunny place. Remove pillow slips or covers and hang affected soft goods from a clothesline for a few hours.

Special advice: Treating pets will not always end a flea problem; a thorough cleanup and treatment of the bed or resting sites is usually required to prevent future outbreaks. Flea larvae feed on animal matter where the host animal normally sleeps. This may be a bed box in the home, a doghouse, or under the front porch. Adult fleas can survive several months without a blood meal from an animal or human.

Helpful hint: Combinations of herbs, brewer's yeast, vitamin B, garlic, ultrasonic collars, herbal shampoos, and herbal collars have not been proven effective in controlling fleas. Flea collars are slow to kill fleas, and don't control fleas on all areas of a pet's body, including near the tail and the back legs where most fleas are found.

•••

112 Cockroaches Inside Home

Problem: Cockroaches are found scavenging inside the home.

Background: Cockroaches, persistent household pests, generally breed in warm, moist, and narrow locations. As scavengers, they will eat almost any food, as well as backing glue, leather, bookbindings, even television wiring. They are nocturnal, hiding during the day and becoming active at night. The cockroaches seen running for cover when the lights are turned on will represent only a small part of the total population; a few seen can indicate a larger population that should be controlled.

Types of cockroaches include the German cockroach, which generally inhabits kitchens or places where food is easily accessible; the Oriental cockroach, which favors warm, humid places, particularly basements; the brown-banded cockroach, which can be found anywhere; the American cockroach, which is found in warm, moist places where food is available; and the wood roach which does not breed indoors, but will invade homes, cabins, and other buildings in or near wooded areas.

What to do: Cockroaches can be carried into homes in bags, boxes, and luggage. Corrugated cardboard boxes can be a source of infestation (see below). To reduce chances of infestation, don't leave food in easily accessible areas, such as pet food in an open bag, or food left in a dish overnight. Keep garbage picked up and stored in closed plastic bags. Fix leaky pipes or faucets. Rinse bottles and store properly. Do not allow boxes, old newspapers, or anything else to clutter rooms and give cockroaches hiding places. Leave spaces between stored packages.

Once an infestation occurs, an insecticide is usually required, along with good sanitation. Several household insecticides available have a long residual effect; apply them where roaches hide or run, such as along baseboards, behind stoves, and along cracks and crevices. It is not necessary to treat flat surfaces, such as countertops or floor surfaces. An infestation in multiple-unit dwellings will probably require the treatment of several units. Cockroaches move along common pipes, electric conduits, and heating ducts. Plug space around these openings to prevent infestation from other units.

Special advice: To avoid moving cockroaches with you, use boxes and packing material from a place uninfested with cockroaches. When packing, watch for cockroaches and their egg capsules, which are dark colored and about the size and shape of a kidney bean. If found, remove and destroy. If boxes are stored overnight in infested buildings, keep them off the floor and away from the walls by placing them on chairs or tables. During the winter, 2 days at 0°F will kill cockroaches at all stages; at 20°F 4 to 5 days may be required, especially for well-insulated boxes.

Helpful hint: When using insecticides, don't spray near food, dishes, or utensils, and don't allow children or pets near treated surfaces until spray has dried. Household aerosol bombs don't deliver enough insecticide to have residual effectiveness against cockroaches. However, pyrethrum aerosols help flush them out and can increase effectiveness of residual pesticides. The use of ultrasonic pest-control devices is not recommended because they have not proven effective.

●●●

113 Snakes Inside Home

Problem: Snakes infest area around the home, or enter home.

Background: Of native wildlife, snakes run a close second to bats as subjects of grim stories, dislike, and misunderstanding. Rattlesnakes can be identified as dangerous by the presence of rattles on the tail. All rattlesnakes are pit vipers and have heat-sensing organs in a small, but readily visible pit, on the side of the head midway between the nostril and the eye. Presence of either the rattle or the pit is a sign the snake is dangerous and should be avoided. All snakes are predators even if they are not venomous.

Small snakes, such as the eastern garter snake, the red-bellied snake, or the prairie ringneck snake feed heavily on worms, snails, slugs, and crawling insects and their larvae. Larger snakes, such as the bullsnake, the plains hognose snake, the timber rattlesnake, and the eastern massasauga, feed on small to medium-sized rodents, including pocket gophers, meadow mice, and brown rats.

What to do: The only long-term control technique that is cost effective is exclusion; there are no commercially available repellents or pesticides registered for use in snake control. Snakes can pass through very small openings, and enter a building near or below ground level. Most snakes do not excavate burrows; they rely on other animals or natural openings. Discourage burrowing rodents from becoming established near buildings. Also keep foundations, sidewalks, driveways, patios, retaining walls, and rock gardens in good shape. Any space around pipes or wires that pass through exterior walls should be sealed. Cover drains or vents with fine-mesh galvanized screens. Keep basement doors and windows tightly screened or closed.

Special advice: When snakes are known to be loose in the house, place moist cloths on the floor in the area where they were last seen. Loosely cover these moist cloths with dry burlap bags or something similar. Check these areas twice a day; snakes like moisture and shelter, and will crawl under or between the folds of these cloths.

Helpful hint: To discourage snakes from residing in your yard, remove as many potential sites for cover as possible, including heavy landscaping, tall grass, flat boards, or rocks. Make lawns around buildings unattractive to snakes by keeping them closely mowed. Always store firewood or lumber away from dwellings.

●●●

114 Bats Inside Home

Problem: Bats become problem around or inside the home.

Background: Bats are the only true flying mammals that also have fur, jaws with teeth, and bear live young. Normally they do not attack humans or fly into their hair. Bats can carry rabies, though few fatalities have occurred due to bites from rabid bats. Another disease problem, histoplasmosis, is associated with some bat colonies. It is caused by inhaling spores or fragments of the naturally occurring soil fungus *Histoplasma capsulatum*. The fungus is most often found in soil enriched by excretions from bats and birds, such as pigeons and starlings. Some infections produce flulike symptoms, though many produce no symptoms or distress.

What to do: Some bat species congregate in colonies. In a building or a home the accumulated odors, droppings, mites, and lice may cause problems. Though persistent, bats have little capacity to chew or scratch through modern building materials. Excluding bats by locating and blocking all entry or exit points is the most cost-effective method of control. Bats enter buildings through various locations, including unprotected vents, broken windows, split siding, chimneys, or other openings. The smallest bats can crawl through openings 3/8-inch wide (or through holes the size of a dime). Locate openings by brightly lighting the inside of potential rest areas at night and observing them from the outside. If this is not possible, observe from the inside on a bright day. Block larger openings with sheet metal or 1/4-inch hardware cloth. Plug narrow cracks with steel wool, oakum, or other packing or insulating material, then seal with an exterior caulk.

Special advice: Be sure all bats are out of the area being bat-proofed before the work is completed. Usually the entire colony will depart from the roosts within 20 or 30 minutes once the first exits, but this may not happen if the bats have been disturbed or harassed. Leave 1 or more well-used exits temporarily open; close after a few days after all bats have departed for the evening. Watch the building at dusk for several days to see if some openings were overlooked.

Helpful hint: There are no effective poison baits for bats because they primarily feed on flying insects. Chemicals may be used to kill bats where all other alternatives fail, though it is expensive and will not provide long-term control.

•••

115 Wasps Around Home

Problem: Wasps have built nests near or around the home.

Background: Wasps can be testy, and sometimes dangerous, pests around the home. In a typical wasp colony, queens are fertilized in fall and hibernate over the winter. At the start of spring, surviving queens start to lay eggs. The first born are workers, which are female with undeveloped ovaries and small wings. Depending on where they are found, workers are the exclusive adult population until about the end of July. About early August, males and queens (larger females able to reproduce and overwinter) emerge, and a colony can often increase tenfold in a matter of months.

What to do: Wasps live in hives which the workers keep building throughout the season. If you find a wasp nest, or see wasps flying near your home, buy an insecticide formulated specifically for them. One insecticide sprays up to 12 feet, kills wasps on contact and has a residual effect that kills wasps returning to the nest, as well as larvae that are not yet fully formed. If you spot a nest, spray it thoroughly so that it is well soaked either at night or early in the morning when adults are inside. (During the day most workers are out of the nest.) Concentrate the spray on the wasp nest, not on solitary wasps in flight.

Special advice: Take special care if the wasp nests are inside wall voids or in the basement or attic of your home. If you discover an outside entrance that wasps are using, do not plug it up. This forces the workers to find another exit. Sometimes, if necessary, they will force their way right into the home. Worker wasps have been known to chew right through wallboard.

Helpful hint: Wasp cycles are irregular; some years they will thrive, other years they will be scarce. Ideal conditions for wasps include a mild winter, followed by a long and moderately moist spring which allows more queens to be produced.

● ● ●

116 Insects Inside Home

Problem: Insects are causing problems within the home.

Background: A long list of chemicals is available for controlling insects that invade the home. However, with the growing concern for the environment and the move away from chemicals, the following are alternative, nonchemical methods of preventing or treating household pests. In most all cases, it's helpful to repair or seal cracks, holes, and other potential points of entry around the home, including foundation, walls, and screens. If the suggestions below don't seem to work, contact your local extension service office or an experienced nursery person.

What to do: For **ants,** use a bait made of 2 parts boric acid in 98 parts food attractant. Select the food attractant by offering ants various materials, such as grease, jelly or peanut butter, and choose the material most frequently selected. For **carpenter ants,** repair moisture-damaged wood. Do not store firewood on the ground, especially near the home. Also keep stored lumber dry. For **carpet beetles and clothes moths,** dry clean or launder clothing before storing. Freeze, dry clean or iron infested articles of clothing. Use mothballs when storing susceptible clothing.

For **centipedes,** eliminate their prey, which is primarily sowbugs. Dry damp areas with a fan or dehumidifier. When found in the home, eliminate with a broom or swatter. For **clover mites,** wipe them up with a damp cloth; they are generally found around windows. Keep 18 inches to 24 inches of soil bordering the home's foundation loose and free of grass. For **crickets,** keep the lawn well mowed and maintain a weed-free area around the home. If using outdoor lights near the home, use a non-attracting yellow light. For **fleas,** keep pets and pet living areas clean; thoroughly vacuum infested rooms (see entry 111).

For **flies,** keep kitchen and other household areas clean. Pour boiling water down drains to eliminate drain-infesting flies. Store garbage in tightly covered receptacles. For **ground beetles,** keep firewood and debris away from the home. When found in the home, remove by hand or by vacuum. For **sowbugs,** reduce moisture through dehumidification. Remove decaying vegetation, such as lawn clippings or fallen leaves, from around the foundation. For **spiders,** keep household areas clean. Eliminate their hiding places and prey (such as sowbugs). When found in the home, kill them using a broom or swatter.

Special advice: For pantry insects, dispose of infested food products. Store uninfested food in tightly sealed glass, metal, or plastic containers. Clean shelves thoroughly, removing crumbs and debris from cracks and crevices. Treat foods more than 60 days old: Foods such as cake mixes and spices in original containers can be cold-treated by exposing them to 0°F (in a freezer) or lower temperatures for 3 to 7 days, depending on the size of package. Dried fruits can be heat-treated by placing them in a cheesecloth bag and dipping them in boiling water for about 6 seconds.

Helpful hint: For **boxelder bugs,** try spraying clustered insects on your home or other buildings with a solution of ½ cup laundry detergent to 1 gallon of water. (Test on an inconspicuous area because detergents discolor some siding.) Vacuum bugs found in the home (properly disposing of the used vacuum bag) or remove them by hand.

● ● ●

117 Insects in Plants or Landscaping

Problem: Insects are found on plants, in gardens, or in landscaping.

Background: Many chemicals are available for controlling the insects that infest outdoor areas around the home. The following suggestions are alternative, nonchemical methods of preventing or reducing many of these pests. If the suggestions don't seem to be effective, contact your local extension service office or an experienced nursery person.

What to do: For **aphids,** remove by dislodging with water spray and spraying with Safers soap solution. Preserve natural predators by protecting ladybugs and lacewings in their immature stage. Plant resistant varieties of honeysuckle which deter witches' broom aphids. For **apple maggots,** remove fallen apples. For a standard-sized tree, hang 8 sticky apple traps, or make them using 3-inch diameter spheres painted bright red or black and coated with a sticky substance such as Tanglefoot or Stickem Special (available in garden centers).

For **cabbage looper** and **imported cabbage worm,** remove caterpillars by hand. Apply *Bacillus thuringiensis,* a natural material available under a variety of product names. For **Colorado potato beetle,** remove immature- and adult-stage insects by hand. Apply *san diego Bacillus thuringiensis,* a natural material. The *san diego* variety is specifically for beetle adults and is available under the name M-ONE. For **cutworms,** place cardboard collars around the transplants, making sure the cardboard extends at least 2 inches above and below the ground (the center core from paper towels works well). Remove cutworms by hand that are hiding in burrows near plants during the day, and those found above ground at night. For **European corn borer** and **corn earworm,** apply *Bacillus thuringiensis.*

For **flea beetles,** control weeds. For **hornworms,** handpick caterpillars and apply *Bacillus thuringiensis.* For **iris borer,** remove old stalks and plant debris in late summer. Remove and destroy infested plants. For **picnic, sap,** and **fungus beetles,** remove damaged and overripe fruit and vegetables. Regularly harvest crops as they ripen. Remove **rose chafers** by hand. Place a cheesecloth barrier around plants as protection during the chafer's flight period in early summer. For **squash vine borer,** slit the plant's stem lengthwise at the point of attack, remove larvae from vines by hand and cover vines with moist soil to encourage new growth.

Special advice: Don't bring infested plants into the home. For plants in the home, remove **caterpillars, slugs** and other pests by hand; for **spider mites,** wash leaves with a mild detergent solution, swab with rubbing alcohol, or spray with Safers soap solution; for **scales** and **mealybugs,** remove with rubbing alcohol or spray with Safers soap solution; for **aphids,** spray plants with a Safers soap solution; for **fungus gnats** and **springtails,** allow soil to dry to a depth of 1 inch before watering; repot plants affected by **millipedes.**

Helpful hint: For **slugs** outdoors, control soil moisture by watering only when necessary; remove by hand. Remove dead leaves and other potential hiding places. Cups filled with beer sunk in the ground will attract and drown slugs. Place boards and shingles on the ground, and remove any slugs attracted to such areas.

● ● ●

118 Wildlife Pests Around Home

Problem: Wildlife causes disturbances or damage in and around home.

Background: With wildlife pests, it is always best to respond to problems as quickly as possible. The longer you wait, the more difficult it will be to change an animal's behavior. The following suggestions are nonchemical methods of dealing with wildlife pests. For more tips on specific problems, contact your local extension service office or an experienced nursery person. Specialized wildlife removal services may also be available in your area to help you deal with wildlife pests humanely; check the telephone directory.

What to do: For **bats,** repair all cracks or holes in the home. Leave the largest hole open for several days. After the bats have left the area in the evening, close up the final opening, but don't do this in early summer when young may be trapped inside the home. (Also see entry 114.) For **deer,** protect individual shrubs and young trees with chicken wire or hardware cloth (a pliable wire screen). Well-built and maintained electric fences are effective for large areas when damage is severe. Use natural repellents on vegetation as soon as damage is observed.

For **mice and rats,** use traps or glue boards. Keep household areas clean and free of food particles. Protect other possible food sources. Repair cracks or holes in the foundation, screens, or other areas where mice and rats may enter the home. For **pigeons,** use sticky substances such as Tanglefoot where pigeons are likely to roost. Use porcupine wire such as Nixalite or Cat Claw to prevent birds from roosting. For **pocket gophers,** trap or periodically cultivate 9 inches to 14 inches of soil to disrupt their burrow system. Live trap **rabbits.** Place cylinders of netting or hardware cloth around individual plants, and use heavy paper or plastic tree wrap around tree trunks. Build a chicken wire fence around the entire garden. For winter protection, apply natural repellents on dormant trees and shrubs. Remove piles of brush, wood, or debris that may provide cover for rabbits.

For **skunks,** close entry points to buildings, and eliminate possible den sites. In severe cases, live trapping may be necessary to eliminate the problem. Live trap **squirrels.** Repair all holes in screens, attic and eave areas, and the foundation of the home. Trim branches of trees that provide access to the roof. For

woodchucks, put an electric fence 5 inches off of the ground and about 5 inches in front of a chicken wire fence that extends 3 feet to 4 feet above the ground and is buried 10 inches to 12 inches in the soil. Live trap or use leg-hold traps.

Special advice: Act quickly if you detect **woodpeckers** eroding the siding of your home or other buildings. Check for, and eliminate, insect problems. Harass birds with water spray. String reflective tape along wall; hang nylon netting from the eaves to the walls to protect damaged areas, and use metal flashing or hardware cloth to protect areas from continued damage.

Helpful hint: Keep in mind that repellents may alleviate a damage problem, but will rarely solve it. For problems with snakes, see entry 113.

TROUBLESHOOTER'S CRISIS GUIDE

The following list describes the basic symptoms of many critical problems that commonly occur in homes. It is intended to help homeowners quickly diagnose the problem, so home emergencies can be resolved before they escalate.

- If an **appliance is on fire,** turn to page 16.

- If a roaring sound is coming from your **chimney** and you think it may be on fire, turn to page 16.

- If you smell a **gaslike odor** in your home, turn to pages 17 and 19.

- If your **gas detector** (an alarm that indicates the presence of gas) sounds, turn to page 18.

- If you are experiencing unexplained headaches, dizziness, drowsiness, nausea, and vomiting, you may have been poisoned by **carbon monoxide** (CO) in your home. Turn to page 20.

- If someone in your home has received an **electrical shock,** turn to page 23.

- If a **tornado** threatens your area, turn to page 25.

- If a **flood** appears imminent, turn to page 26.

- If a **hurricane** is forecast for your area, turn to page 29.

- If a strong **earthquake** has struck your area, turn to page 31.

- If someone in your home is experiencing a sudden loss of appetite, irritability, constipation, headaches, stomach cramps, drowsiness, sleep loss, lethargy, or loss of recently acquired skills, you may have an unsafe level of **lead** in your home. In homes built before 1960, lead pipes (common before 1930), and copper pipes joined with lead-based solder (common before 1980) are the most likely sources of lead. Turn to page 39.

- If your **toilet** appears to be plugged, turn to page 57.

- If your **pipes** appear to have frozen, turn to page 68.

- If your **furnace** will not work, even when the thermostat is raised, turn to page 82.

- If your **furnace** is making unfamiliar noises, turn to page 83.

- If your **water heater** makes sizzling, popping, or rumbling noises, turn to pages 91, 92, and 93.

- If you live in a region that has severe winter weather and notice that your insulation is soaked, the paint is peeling inside and outside the house, or that you have damp, musty-smelling wall cavities, the problem may be **ice dams.** Turn to page 141.

- If your manually or automatic-operated **garage door** will not operate properly, turn to pages 146, 147, and 148 before attempting to make any adjustments.

GLOSSARY

Ampere: Unit of measure for the rate of flow of electrical energy *(see volt)*; watts divided by volts equals amperes.

Anode rod: Device used inside water heaters to protect the tank against corrosion.

Auxiliary heaters: Heating devices used in addition to the main heating system, such as kerosene heaters, fireplaces, or electrical space heaters.

Awning window: A window that cranks out at the bottom by turning a crank handle; can provide ventilation even in rainy weather.

Basin wrench: Long tool with a flexible, self-gripping head that is used to turn hard-to-reach nuts that hold basins and faucets in place.

Blast bag: Slang term for hydraulic drain openers which are attached to a garden hose and pulsate under high water pressure.

Blower: In reference to forced, warm-air furnaces, the centrifugal fan driven by an electric motor that draws cold air from rooms through the cold-air ducts into the furnace and then forces warmed air back to the rooms through the hot-air ducts.

Blower belt: The V-belt which is used to link an electric motor to a centrifugal fan used in a forced, warm-air furnace.

Casement window: Hinged at one side, and may swing out or in as it is cranked by a handle.

Caulking: Procedure of sealing or weatherproofing cracks between materials; may also refer to the caulk material used, such as silicone caulking.

Closet auger: Special, flexible version of a clean-out auger designed for use in toilets; has protective tubing to protect ceramic toilets from scratches.

Cord clamp: Metal clamp with screws on the exterior of larger replacement plugs which is used to secure the cord to the plug.

Condensor switch: In air-conditioning systems, an additional switch that directly controls the motor which powers the fan and the compressor in a unit which is usually located outdoors.

Cotter pin: A hairpin-like fastener which is inserted through a hole (in a shaft, for example) with its two leg sections spread open to hold it in place.

Crocus cloth: Has powdered iron oxide on cloth backing; generally used for polishing.

Circuit breaker panel: Term for main service panel housing the main switches and branch circuits protected by circuit breakers. If circuits become overloaded, a circuit breaker trips to interrupt electrical flow to that circuit *(see fuse box)*.

Cylinder lockset: Used on exterior doors; locked by key inserted into a cylinder within the outside knob, or with turn knob or push button on inner knob.

Double-hung window: Divided into two sections that ride in channels in the jamb on both sides; the top sash can be lowered, the bottom sash can be raised.

Drain cock: A faucet-like device that is turned to allow liquid to drain.

Drain (or disposal) field: A system of underground drain pipe in a private sewer disposal system which is connected to a septic tank through a distribution box.

Drive belt: The flexible V-belt which transfers power between motors and driven devices *(see blower belt)*.

Drywall: Generic term for gypsumboard used in place of lath and plaster to cover walls;

Sheetrock is a brand name. May also be called wallboard or plasterboard.

Drywall tape: Narrow strips used, along with joint compound, to finish joints in sections of drywall; may be made of paper or perforated paper without adhesive, or of fiberglass with adhesive backing.

Drywell: A device used to catch and hold water; may be a metal drum sunken into the ground, filled with rocks, and connected to drains to collect rainwater runoff.

Electrical conduit: Metal pathways that carry electric wires; may be greenfield (also known as flexible metal conduit), electric metallic tubing conduit (EMT), or BX cable (also known as armored cable, Type A.C.)

Electronic ignition: In a furnace, an electronic device which provides a direct spark to the main burner, eliminating the need for a pilot burner.

Emery cloth: Has emery abrasive, a natural mineral, on cloth backing; used for rust removal or for sanding metal.

Expansion nozzle: Another term for a hydraulic drain opener, a balloon-type device which connects to a garden hose and is inserted into clogged drains.

Faceplate: The metal plate surrounding the latchbolt that is inset into the door on the latch side.

Feathering: Gradual tapering of added material, such as drywall compound, over a distance so that changes in surface thickness are not noticeable.

Flat-wire plug: Electrical plug designed to accept wires that are flat, as opposed to wires that are round.

Float valve: A valve that opens and closes to keep water at a specific level in a container; generally actuated by the up-and-down movement of a float on the water's surface.

Flywheel: A wheel of sufficient mass attached to a shaft to help provide continuous momentum.

Forced-air furnace: A furnace which heats and distributes air to the home using a fan to draw cooled air from the rooms through cold-air ductwork to the furnace heating chamber, and back to rooms through hot-air ducts.

Four-way switch: Used in combination with three-way switches when power must be turned on and off from more than two locations.

Fuse box: Term for main service panel that houses the main switches and branch circuits protected by fuses; if circuits become overloaded, a fuse burns out to interrupt electrical flow to that circuit (*see circuit breaker panel*).

Glider window: Windows that can be opened and closed by sliding sections horizontally.

Ground-fault circuit interrupter (GFCI): Special receptacle or circuit breaker which detects current flow changes and quickly shuts off before shocks can occur; used in circuits supplying power to outlets in baths, kitchens, laundry rooms, or outdoors.

Gypsumboard: A term used for wallboard (*see drywall*).

Hard-wired: Electrical-powered device which is wired directly into the electrical system of the home, as opposed to one that draws power from a plugged-in power cord or batteries.

Jalousie window: Consists of several narrow horizontal glass sections that pivot in unison for either opening or closing when a hand crank is turned.

Joists: Horizontal wood members that support either floors or ceilings.

Kilowatt: Equal to 1,000 watts; watts divided by 1,000 equals kilowatts. One kilowatt working for one hour equals one kilowatt-hour (kwh).

Media pad: In a home humidifier, the thin, fibrous material that picks up water to be evaporated; may be a smaller pad wrapped around a wheel framework in a central humidifier, or a larger, wider pad running over rollers in a portable humidifier.

Media wheel: In a home humidifier, the wheel-shaped framework that holds the media pad material in place *(see media pad)*.

O-ring: Rubberbandlike ring, generally round in cross-section, which fits between two components to provide a seal.

Octopus plug: A special plug that allows several more plugs to be inserted; its use is ordinarily not recommended by safety specialists and electricians.

Oil heating system: System employing a furnace or stove that burns fuel oil; may be a forced-air system with a blower or a system that depends on the rise of warm air.

Packing nut: A nut with an interior recess that accepts packing material to help seal in a liquid, such as water or oil.

Pilot burner: Small flame that ignites a flame in main burners when fuel is turned on in appliances such as furnaces, water heaters, or kitchen ranges.

Plumber's friend: Plunger with rubber cup on the end of a wooden handle, used to unclog fixture drains by vigorously moving up and down.

Plumbing fixture: A receptacle, such as a sink, basin, or toilet, that is connected to the plumbing

system and collects and retains water or wastes for discharge.

Plumbing stack: Main vent into which all fixtures drain; it is also the vent pipe which emerges through the roof of the house.

Plumbing trap: Special curved fitting needed under all fixtures except toilets to prevent sewer gas from entering the home. Toilets have built-in traps.

Pressure-reducing valves: Special valves that reduce pressure sometimes employed in homes to lower pressure from water mains for use inside the home.

Quick-connect plug: Electrical plug connected by inserting the wires, with spikes making contact between the prongs of the plug and the wires.

Rafters: Sloping wooden members that support the roof of a home.

Receptacle: In electrical systems, outlets within electrical boxes mostly in walls and floors that accept plugs; the most common are those with openings for two plugs, called duplex receptacles; also sometimes referred to as plug-ins.

Replacement plug: Electrical plug, available in several varieties, designed to replace original plugs or other replacement plugs that have become defective.

Roof louvers: Series of slanted slots allowing for ventilation while repelling rain.

Roof vents: Openings that allow attic air to exit through the roof; may be assisted by power fans or wind-assisted turbine devices over the vent. Ridge vents are nonmechanical vents installed along the roof ridge.

Romex: Nonmetallic-sheathed electrical cable which can be used without metal raceways *(see electrical conduit).*

Round-cord plug: Electrical plug designed to accept wires that are round instead of flat.

Seat wrench: A special L-shaped tool used to remove a faucet seat; the seat mates with a washer fastened to the handle stem that is turned to close off the water supply.

Set-back thermostats: Programmable thermostats which save energy by automatically dropping the temperature setting for specific periods during heating seasons, or by raising the temperature settings during certain periods during the cooling season.

Sheetrock: Brand name for wallboard *(see drywall).*

Shims: Narrow strips of wood or other material used to increase thickness; common wood shims used in homes are thin at one end and thicker at the other, and are driven between adjoining wood members.

Single-pole switch: A switch that turns power on and off from only one point.

Soffit vents: Openings within the soffits (the underside of the roof overhang on the outside of the home).

Solenoid: Electronic device that moves on command to allow, for example, the opening and closing of valves.

Spiraled auger: A flexible "plumber's snake" often made of coiled spring material with its working end configured in spiraling, hooklike manner.

Spline: Slotted grooves, usually on a shaft, designed to accept a second part with corresponding ridges and slots.

Strikeplate: The metal plate used around the hole in the doorjamb that accepts the latchbolt of a door lockset.

Subflooring: First layer of flooring material which lies directly over the floor joints; may be diagonal rough boards or plywood.

Sump pump: An electrically powered pump which is positioned in a "sump" or hole to pump out collected water when it reaches a certain level.

Temperature-pressure relief valve: Special valve used on water heaters that automatically opens before an increase in temperature or pressure could cause an explosion.

170

THE HOME REPAIR EMERGENCY HANDBOOK

Terminal clips: Clips that are flat in configuration and that slip over prongs to make an electrical connection.

Three-way switch: Switch used in pairs to switch power on and off from two different locations.

Tilt-turn window: Newer style which tilts in at the top to provide ventilation and can turn a full 180° for easy cleaning.

Trip lever: Device used to initiate operation of mechanisms (such as the handle on the tank of a toilet) that begins the flushing operation when pushed.

Tubular lockset: Mostly used in interior doors. May have a push button in its knob or a small lever or button on its interior side.

Underwriter's knot: A special knot used when replacing plugs or cords (where space allows) to help reduce tension on wires connected to screw terminals.

Volt: Unit of measure for electrical pressure; volts times amperes equals watts or, expressed differently, (pressure) times (current flow) equals power.

Water-mixing valve: A device that mixes hot and cold water to produce water of specific temperatures.

Water-resistant gypsumboard: Drywall sheets with a water-resistant paper wrapper for use in areas of high humidity.

Watt: Unit of measure for electrical energy. One ampere of current flow at a pressure of one volt equals one watt of electrical energy (*see ampere and volt*).

X-bridging: The wood or metal braces used between joists to brace one joist to the next to prevent twisting.

INDEX